my bird book

name _____

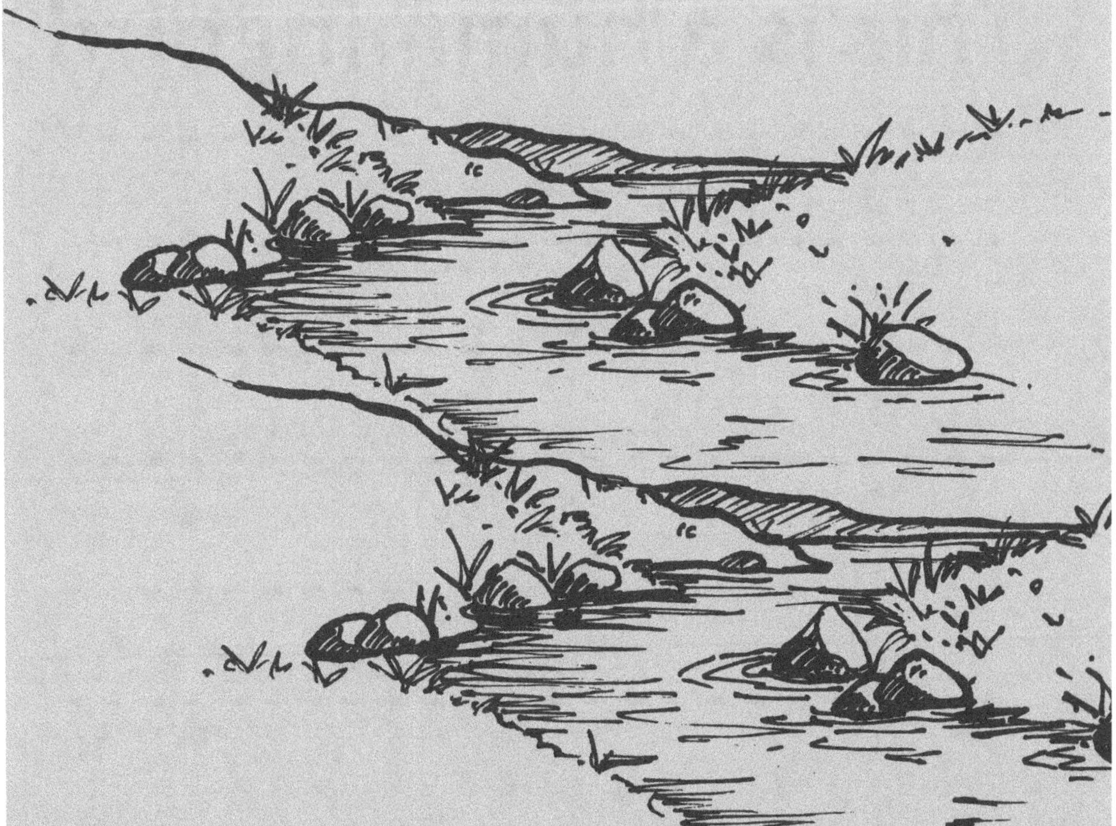

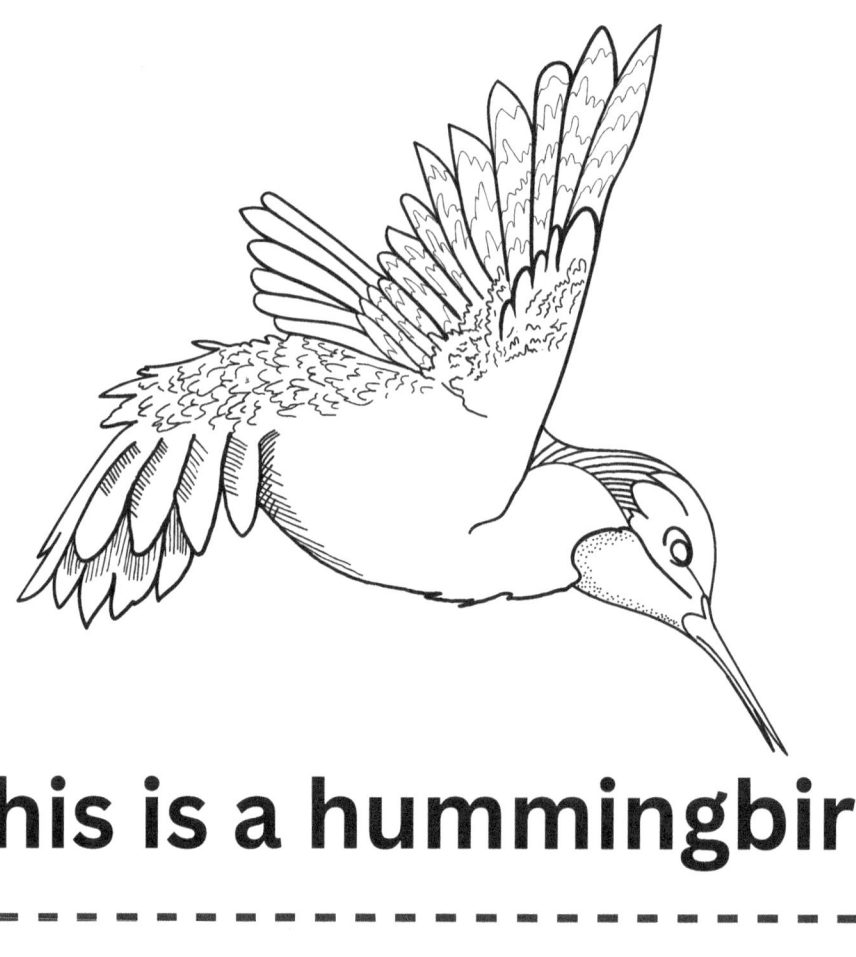

This is a hummingbird

- -

- -

- -

- -

- -

- -

This is a hummingbird

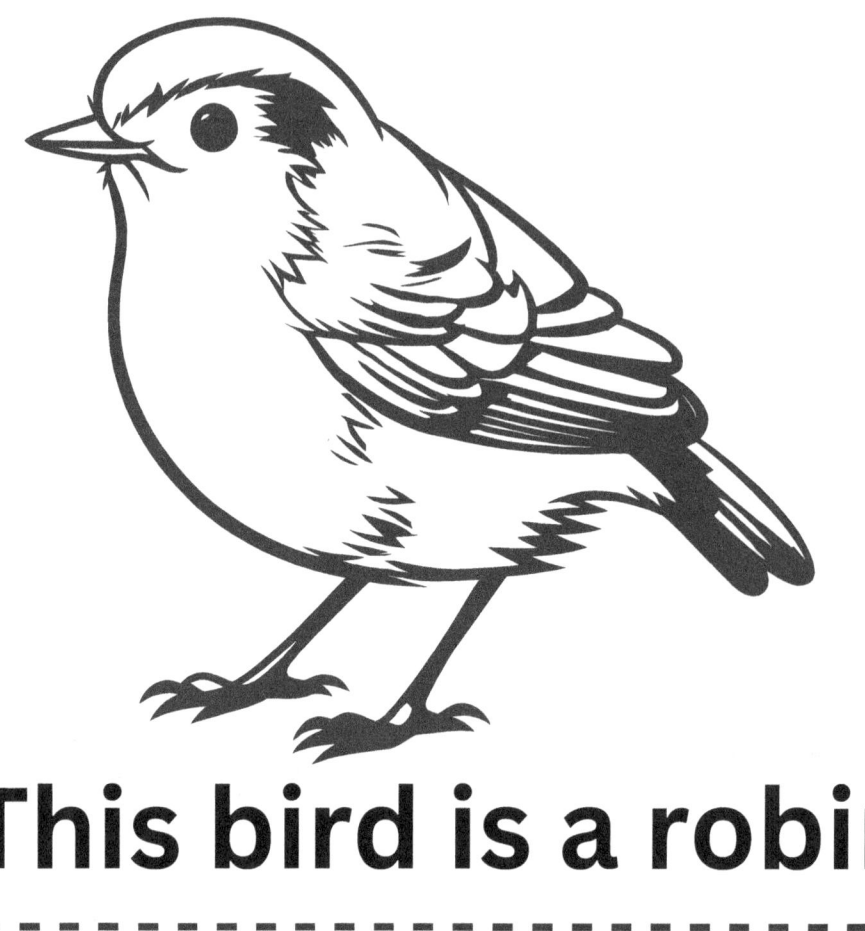

This bird is a robin

- -

- -

- -

- -

- -

- -

This bird is a robin

- -

- -

- -

- -

- -

- -

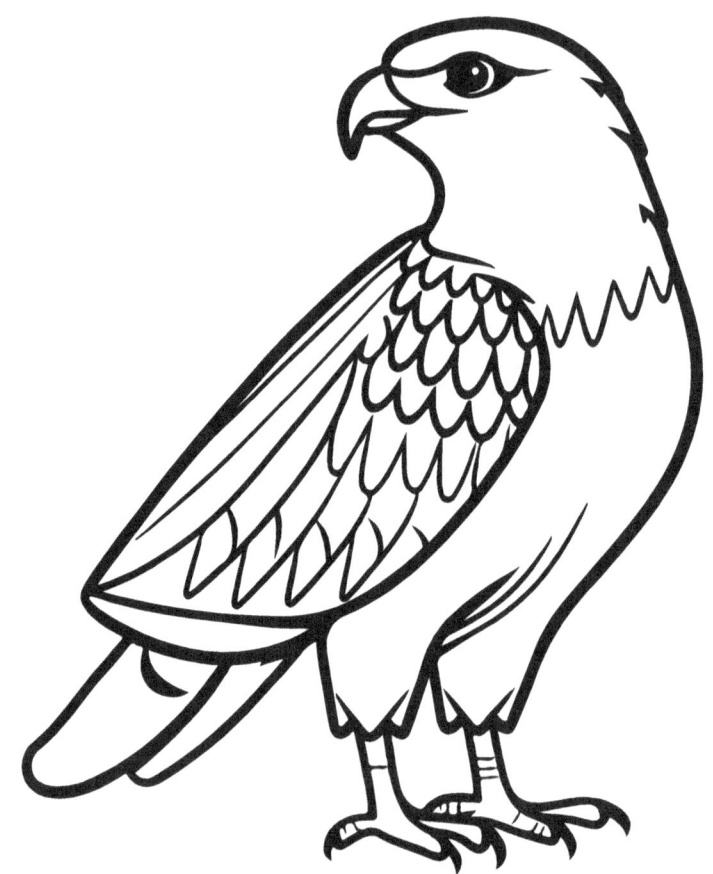

This bird is a hawk

- -

- -

- -

- -

- -

- -

This bird is a hawk

- -

- -

- -

- -

- -

- -

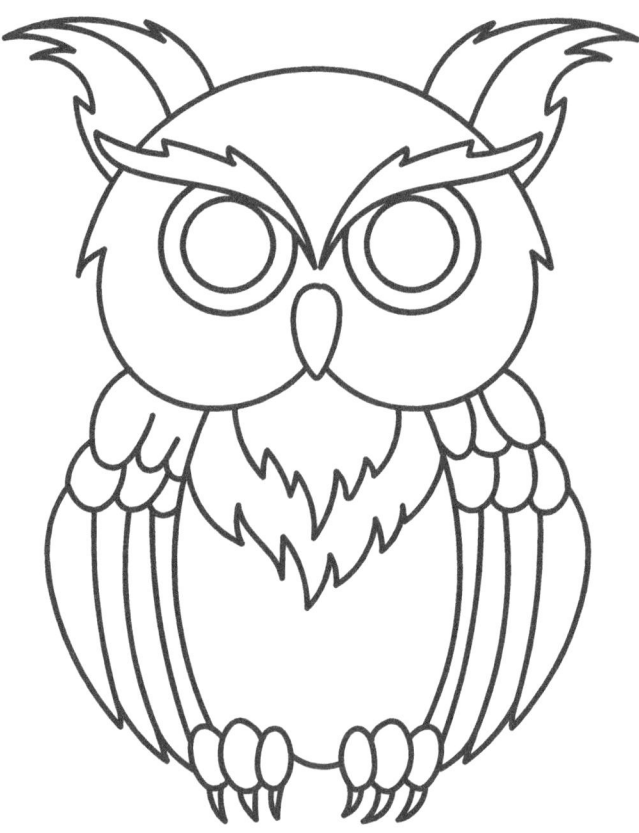

This bird is called an owl

This bird is called an owl

- -

- -

- -

- -

- -

- -

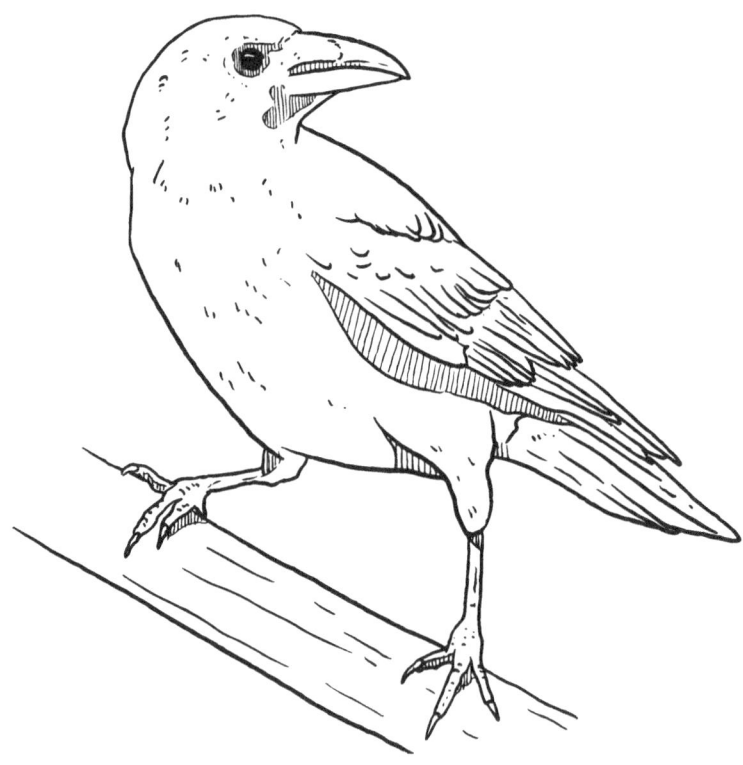

this bird is called a crow

- -

- -

- -

- -

- -

- -

this bird is called a crow

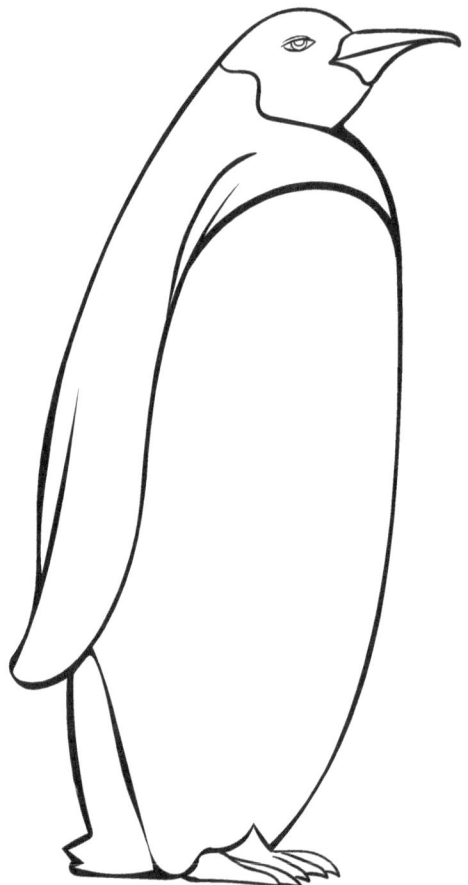

This bird is called a penguin

- -

- -

- -

- -

- -

This bird is called a penguin

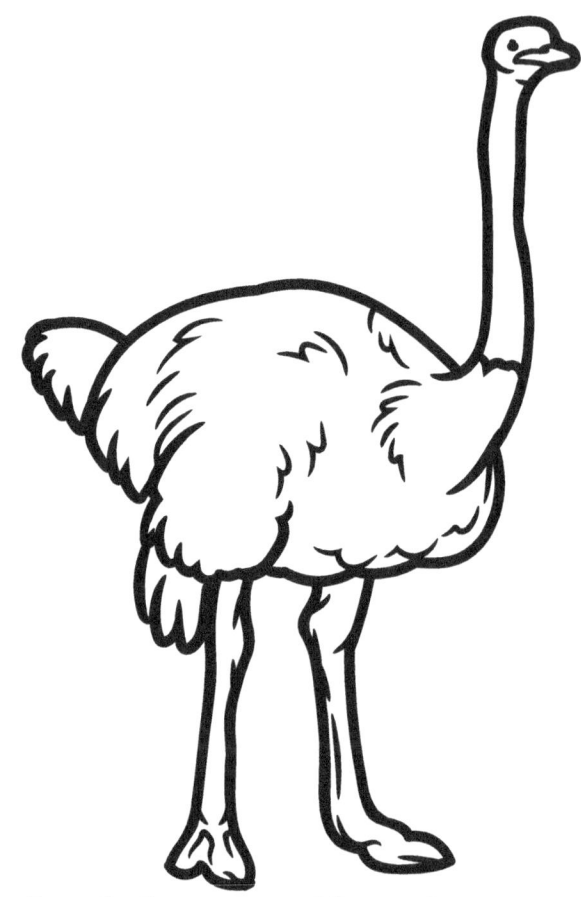

This bird is called an ostrich

This bird is called an ostrich

- -

- -

- -

- -

- -

- -

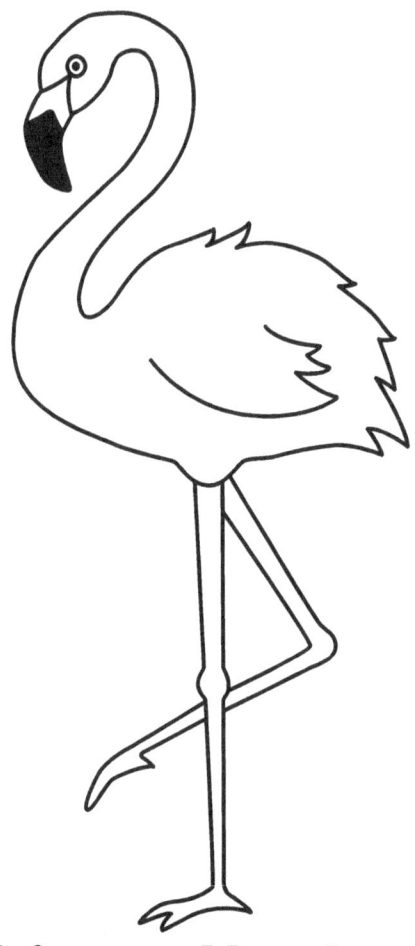

This bird is called a flamingo

- -

- -

- -

- -

- -

This bird is called a flamingo

- -

- -

- -

- -

- -

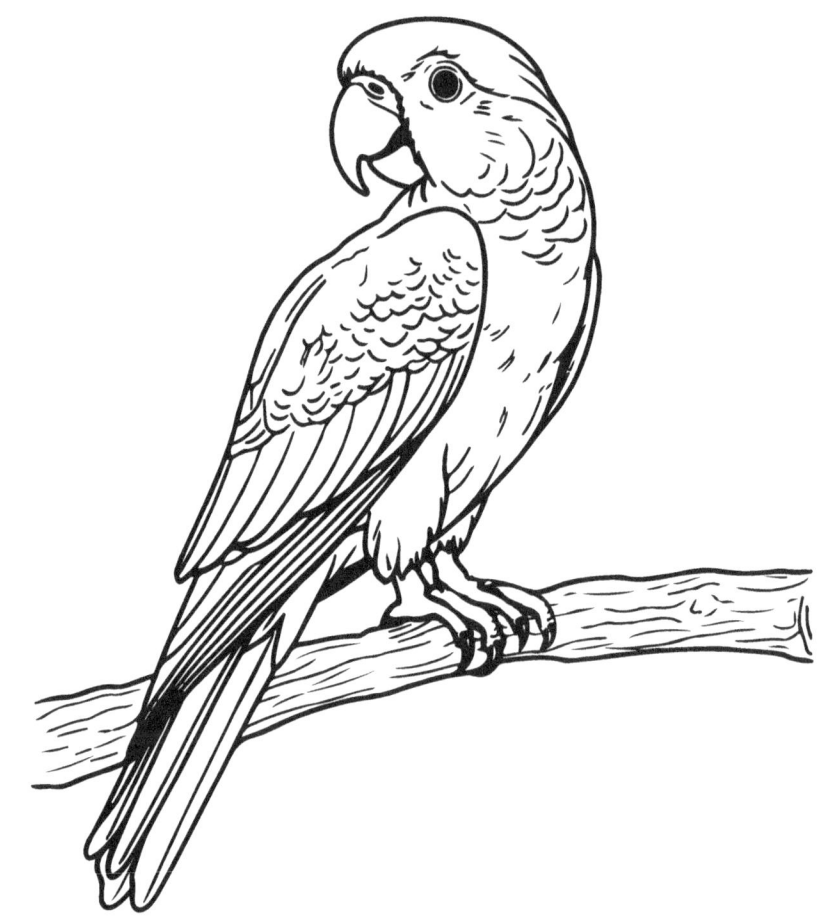

This bird is called a parrot

- -

- -

- -

- -

- -

This bird is called a parrot

- -

- -

- -

- -

- -

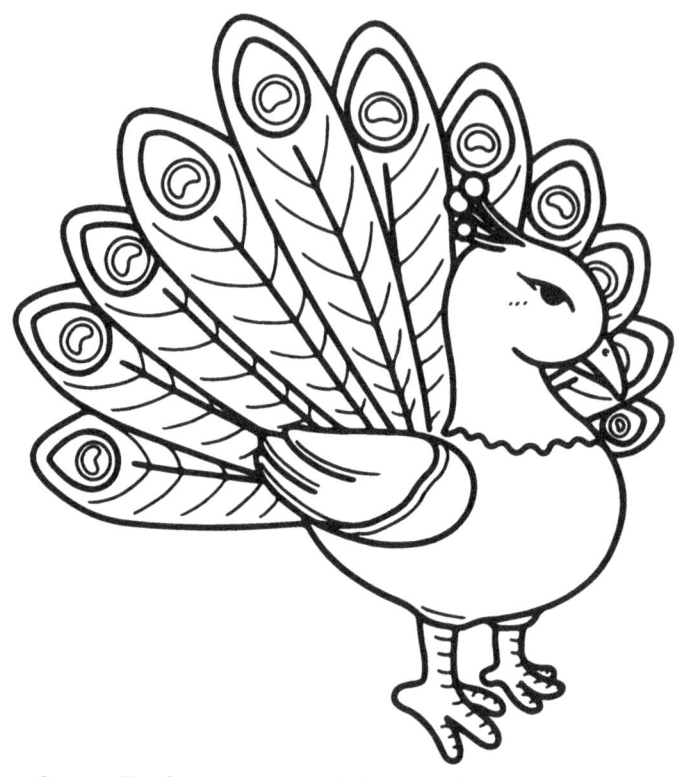

This bird is called a peacock

- -

- -

- -

- -

- -

- -

This bird is called a peacock

- -

- -

- -

- -

- -

- -

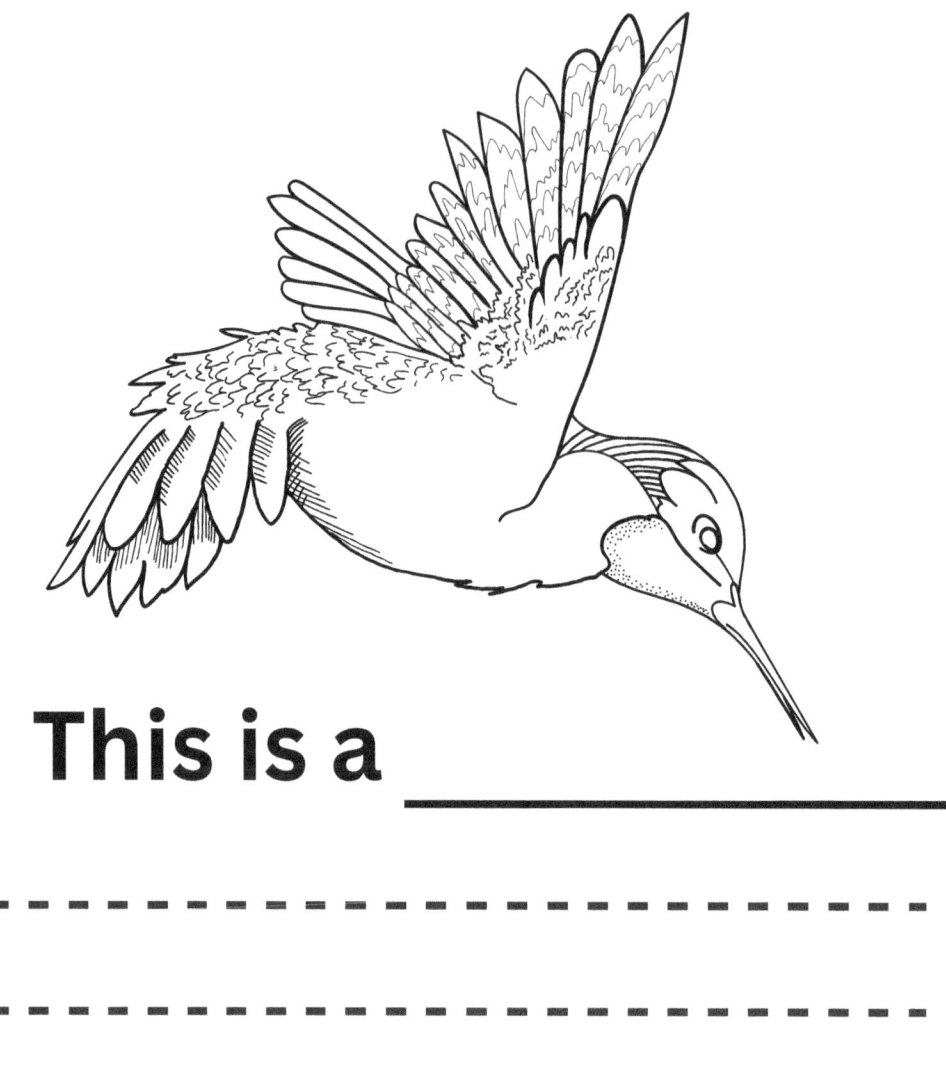

This is a _____

- -

- -

- -

- -

- -

- -

This is a _____

- -

- -

- -

- -

- -

- -

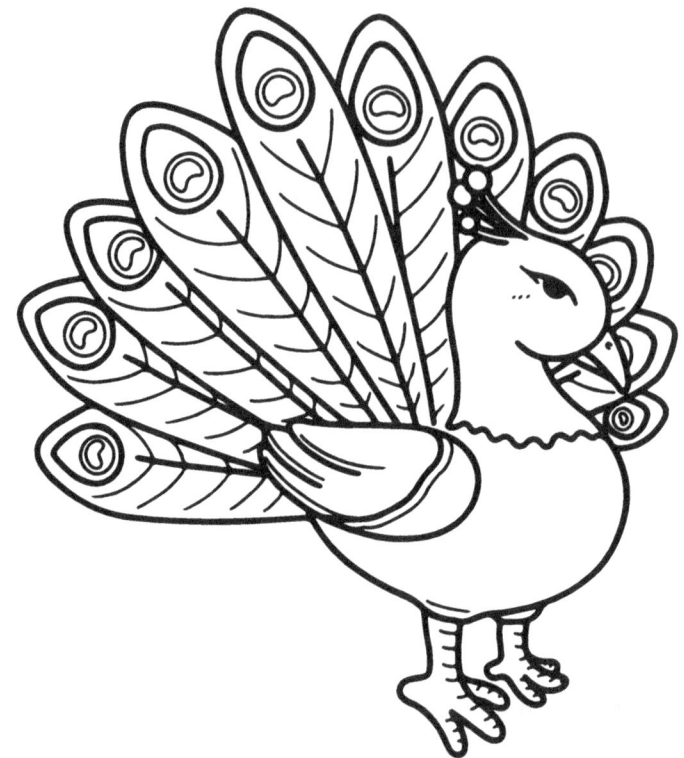

This bird is called a _____

- -

- -

- -

- -

- -

- -

This bird is called a _____

- -

- -

- -

- -

- -

- -

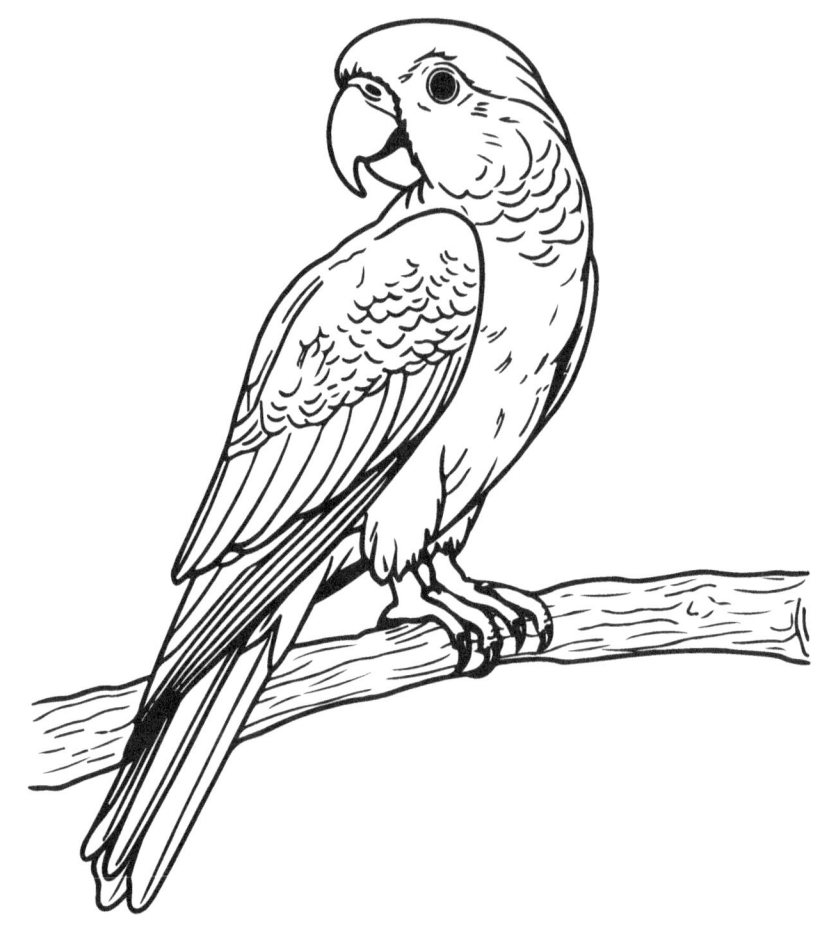

This bird is called a _____

- -

- -

- -

- -

- -

This bird is called a _____

- -

- -

- -

- -

- -

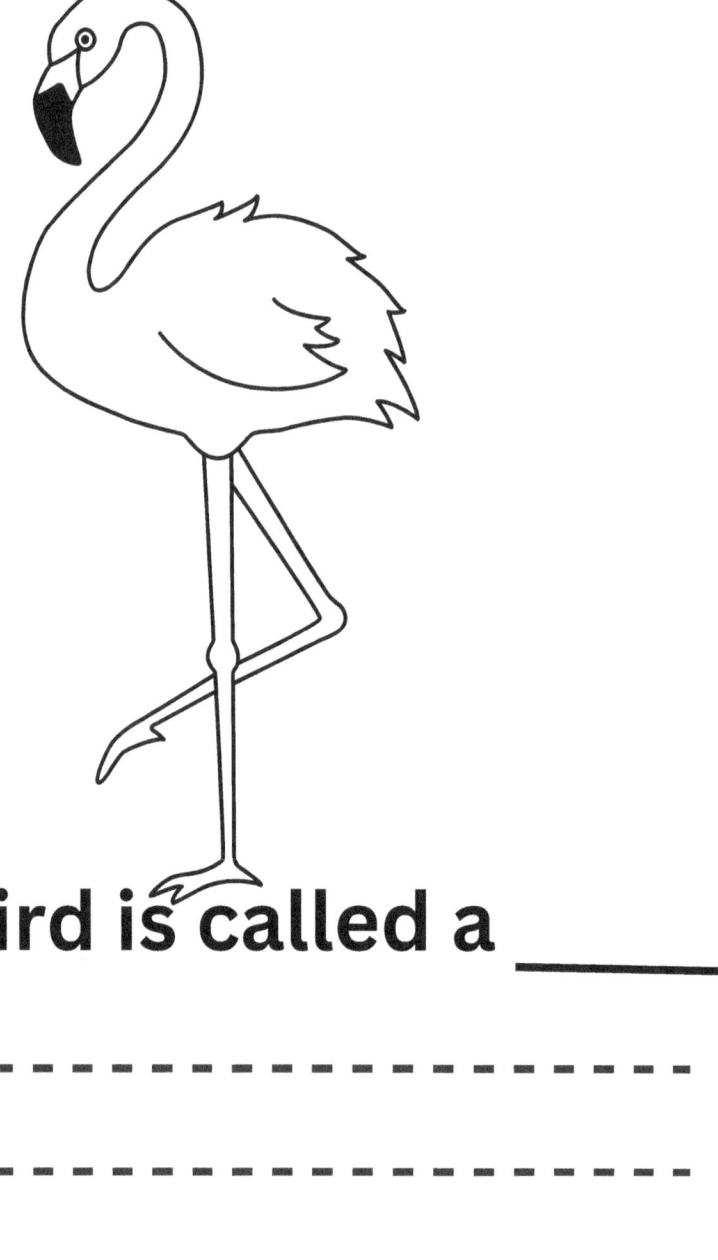

This bird is called a _____

- -

- -

- -

- -

- -

This bird is called a _____

- -

- -

- -

- -

- -

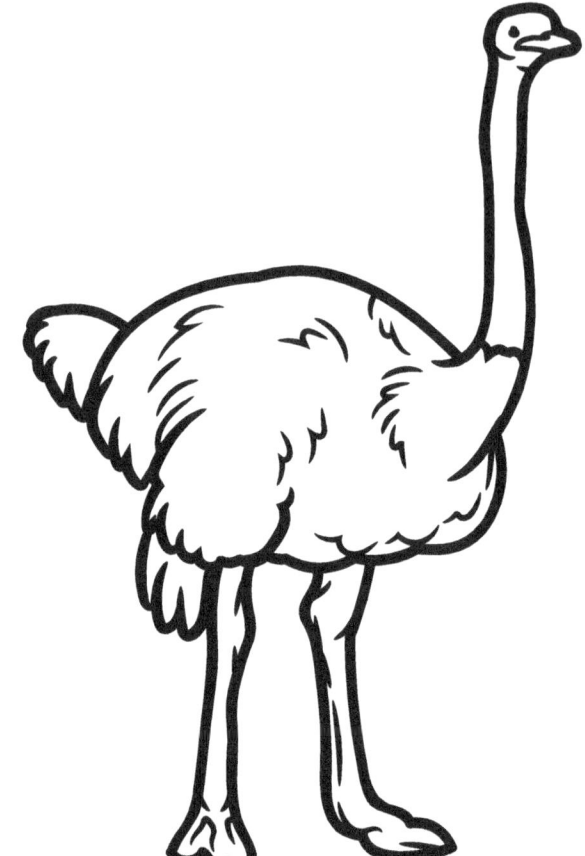

This bird is called a _____

- -

- -

- -

- -

- -

- -

This bird is called a _____

- -

- -

- -

- -

- -

- -

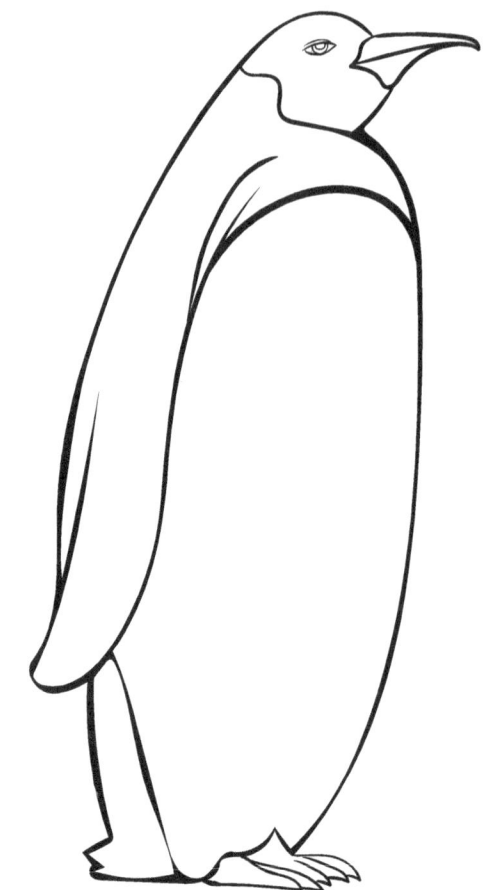

This bird is called a _____

- -

- -

- -

- -

- -

This bird is called a _____

- -

- -

- -

- -

- -

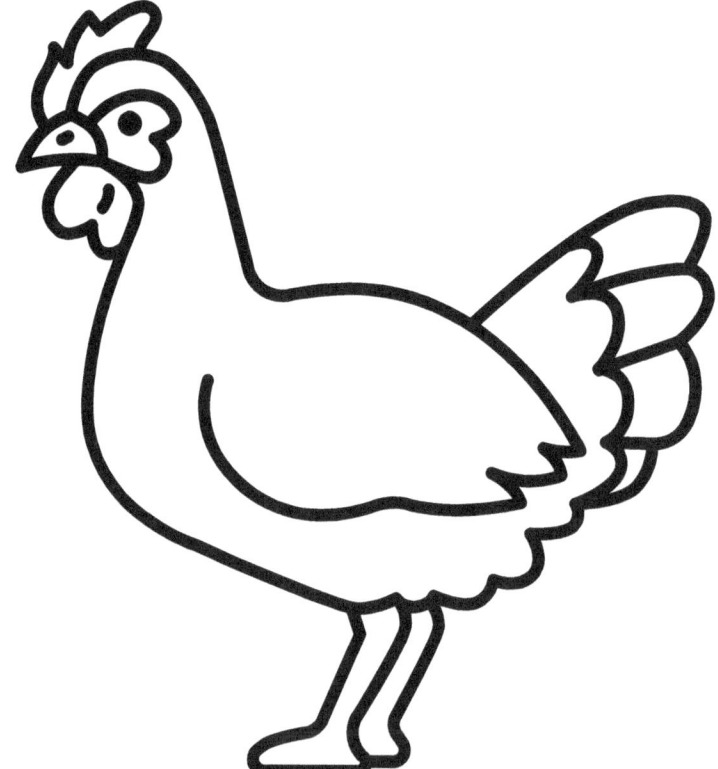

This bird is called a _____

- -

- -

- -

- -

- -

- -

This bird is called a _____

- -

- -

- -

- -

- -

- -

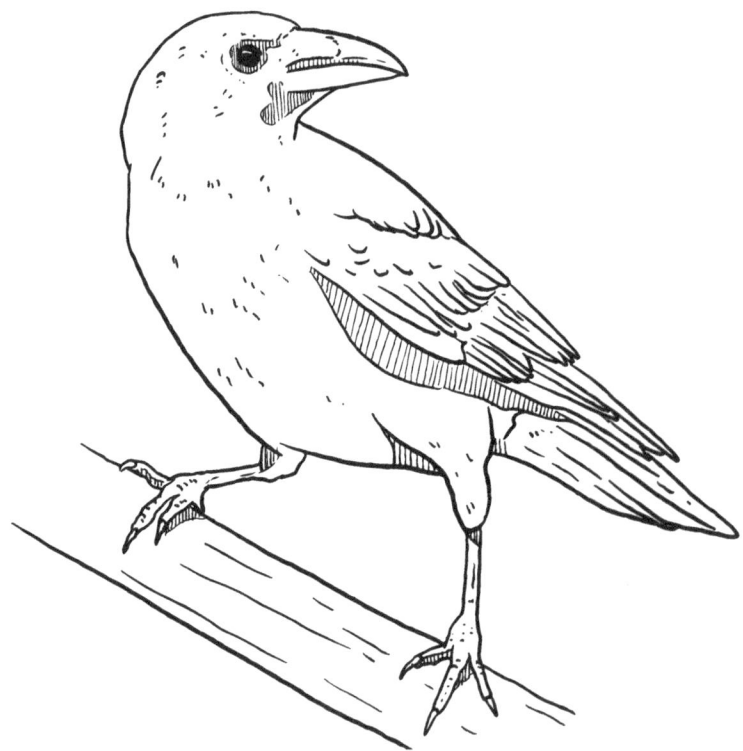

this bird is called a _____

this bird is called a _____

- -

- -

- -

- -

- -

- -

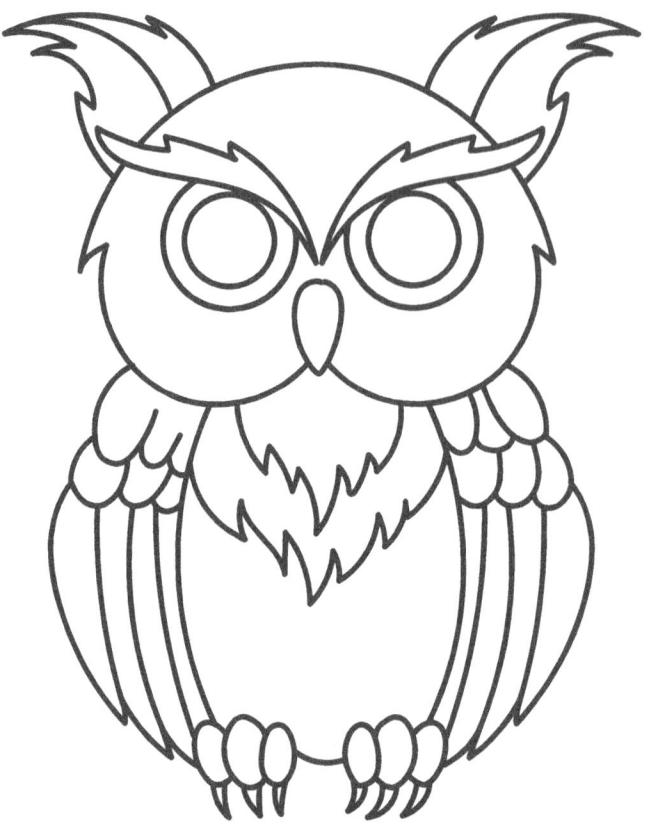

This bird is called a _____

- -

- -

- -

- -

- -

- -

This bird is called a _____

- -

- -

- -

- -

- -

- -

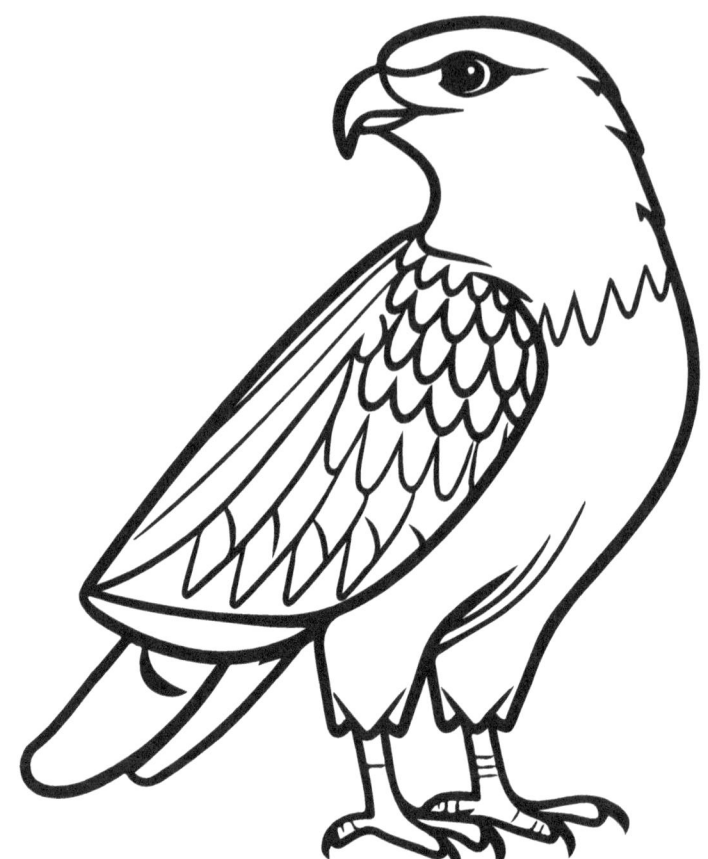

This bird is a ___

- -

- -

- -

- -

- -

- -

This bird is a ___

- -

- -

- -

- -

- -

- -

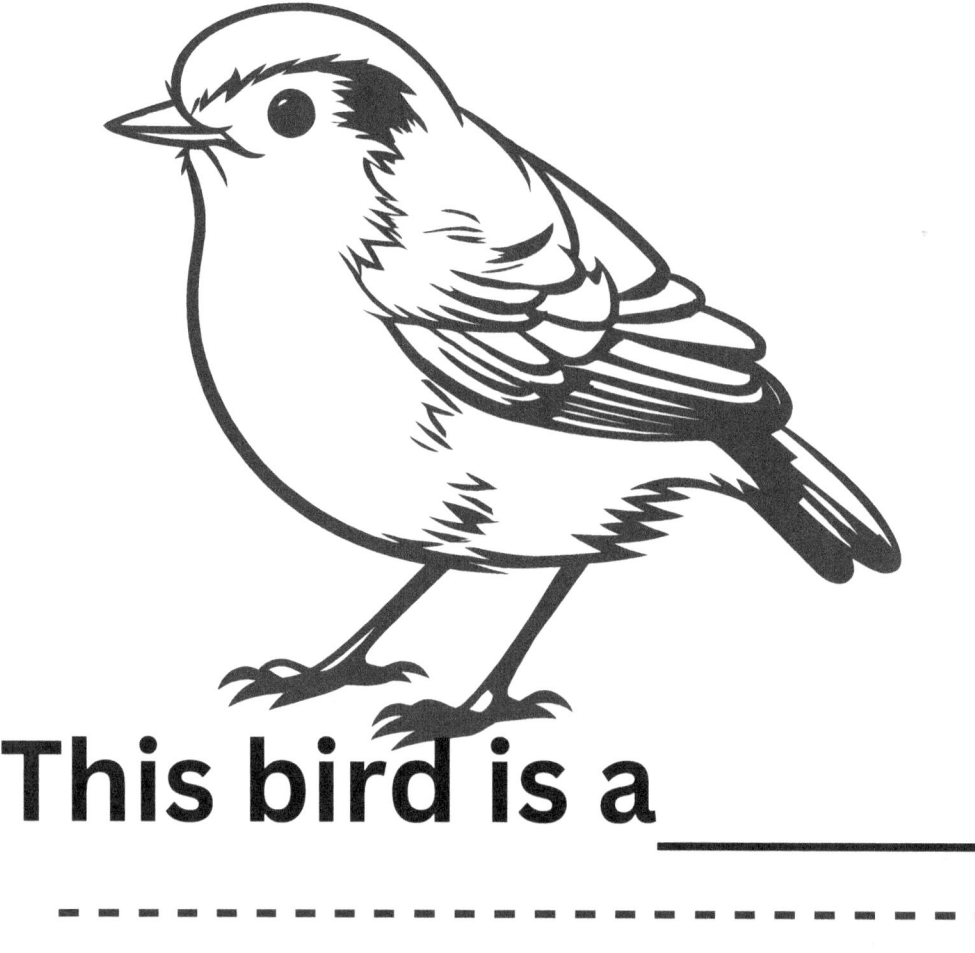

This bird is a _____

- -

- -

- -

- -

- -

- -

This bird is a_____

- -

- -

- -

- -

- -

- -

Observations about birds

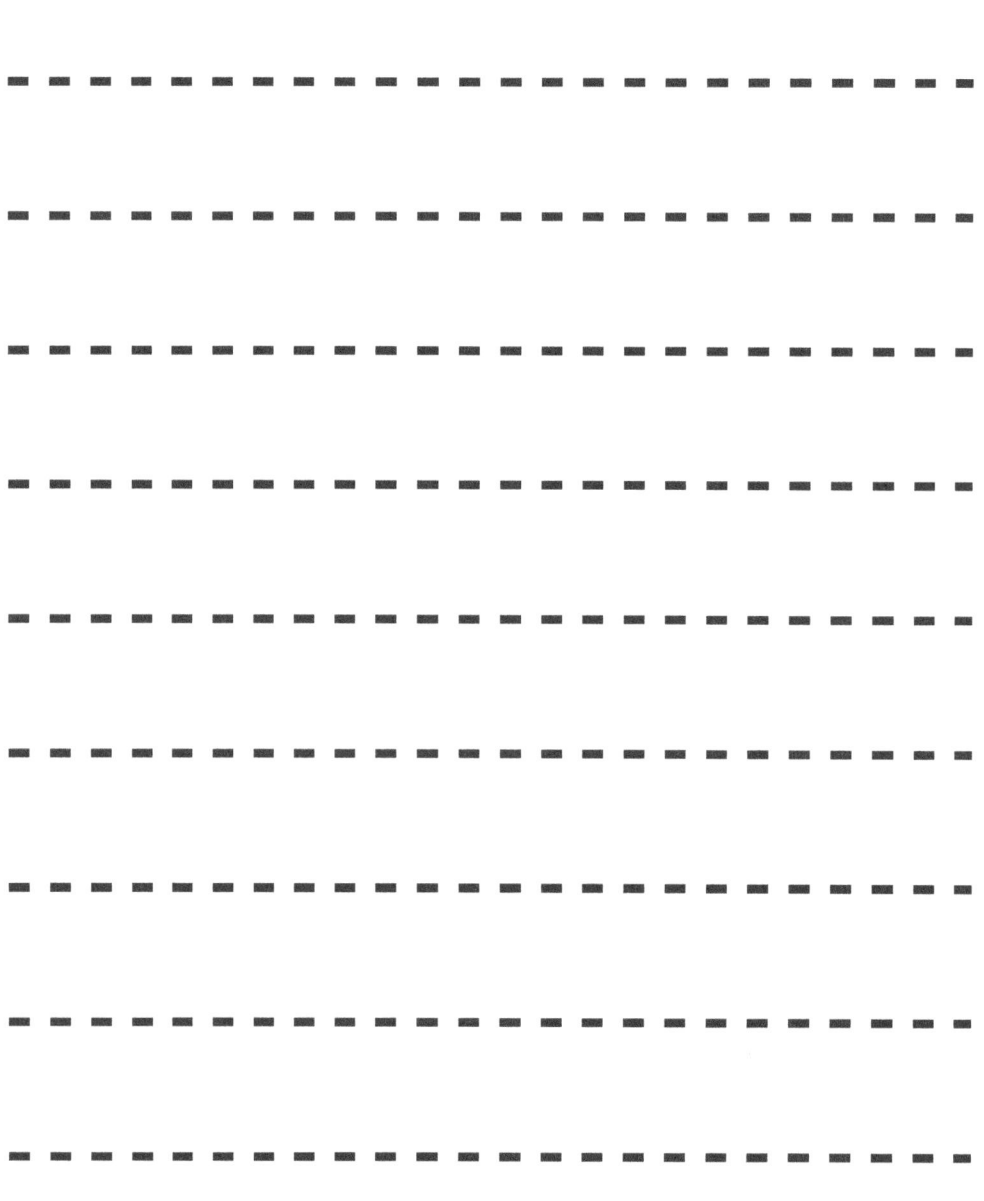

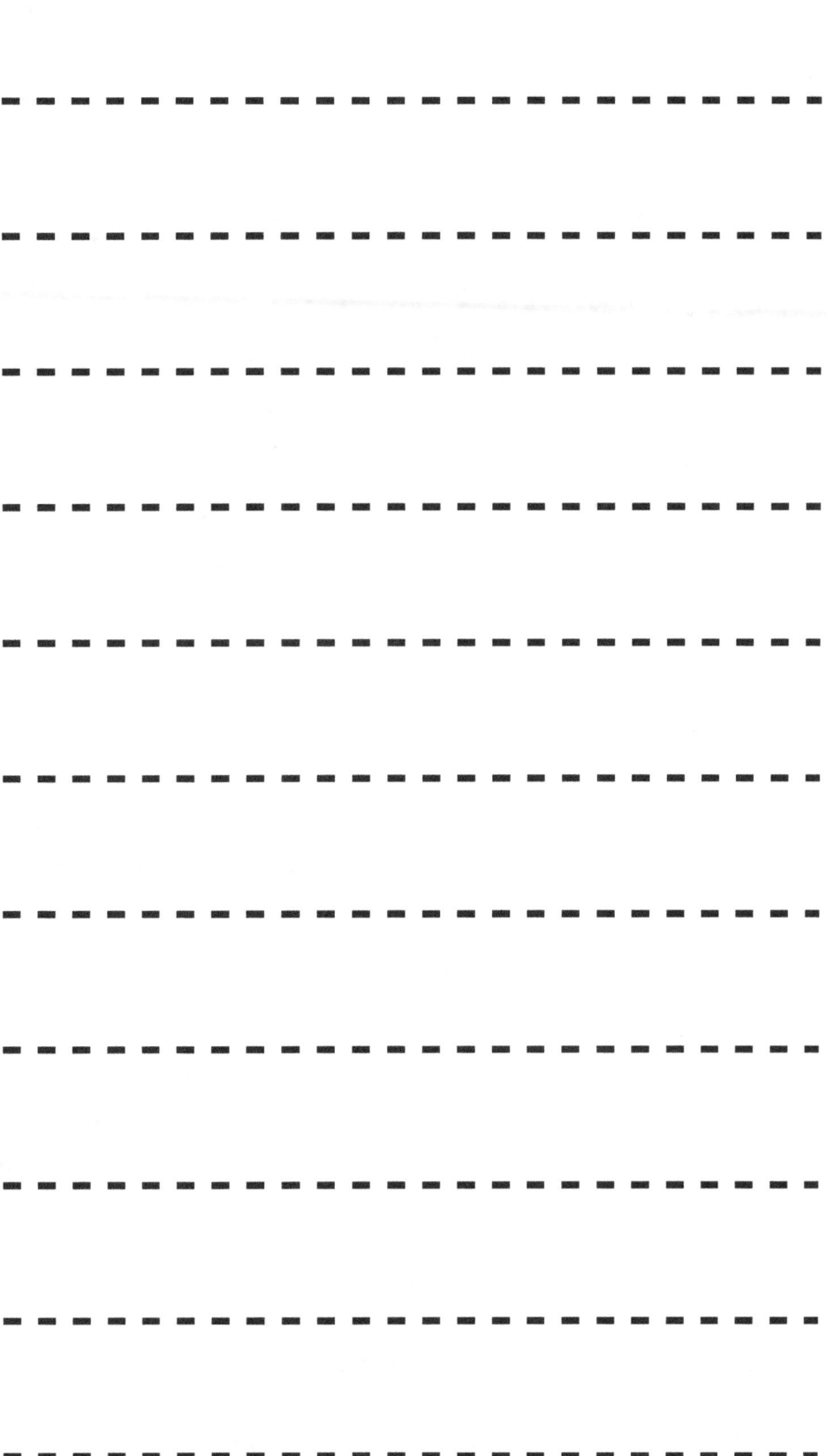

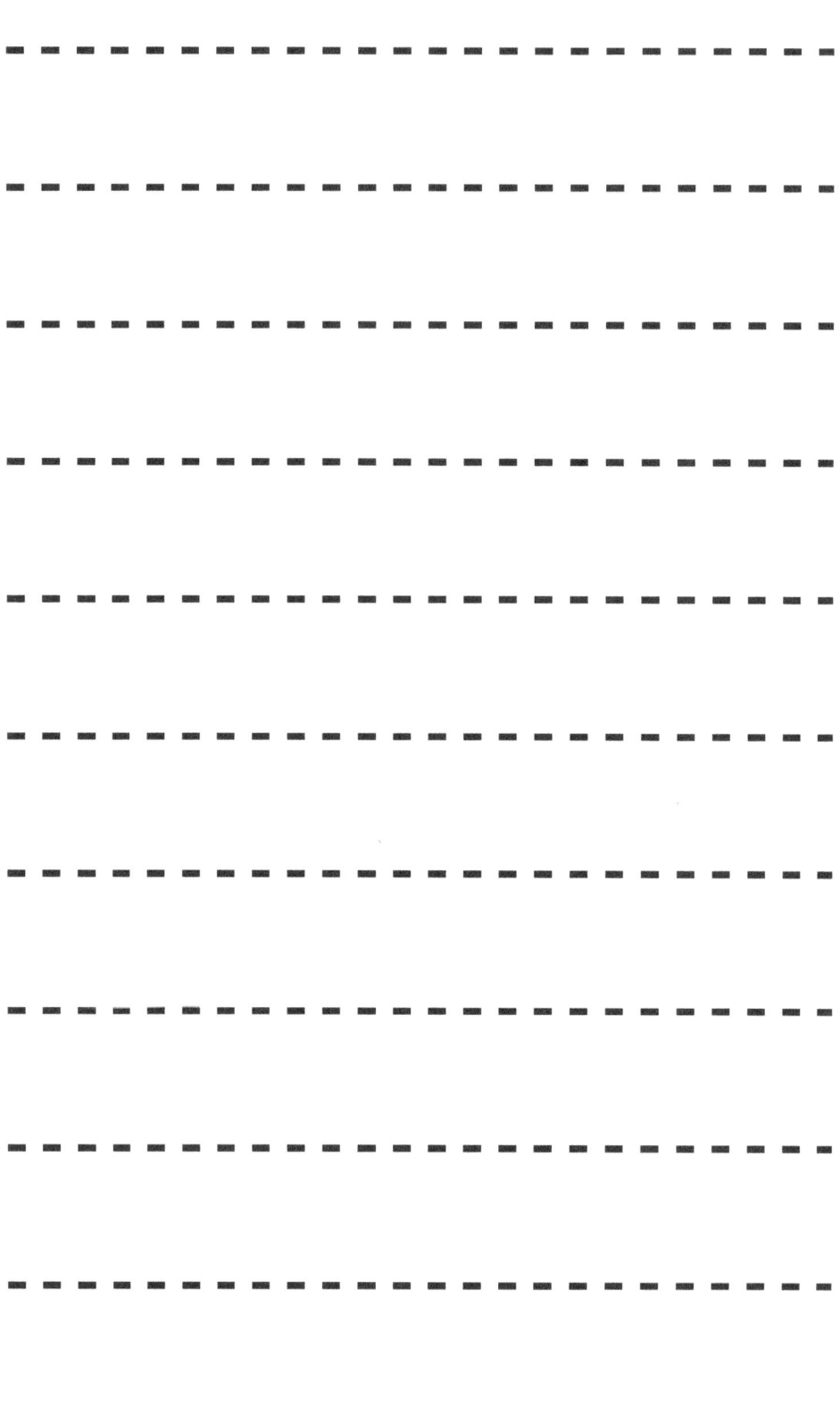

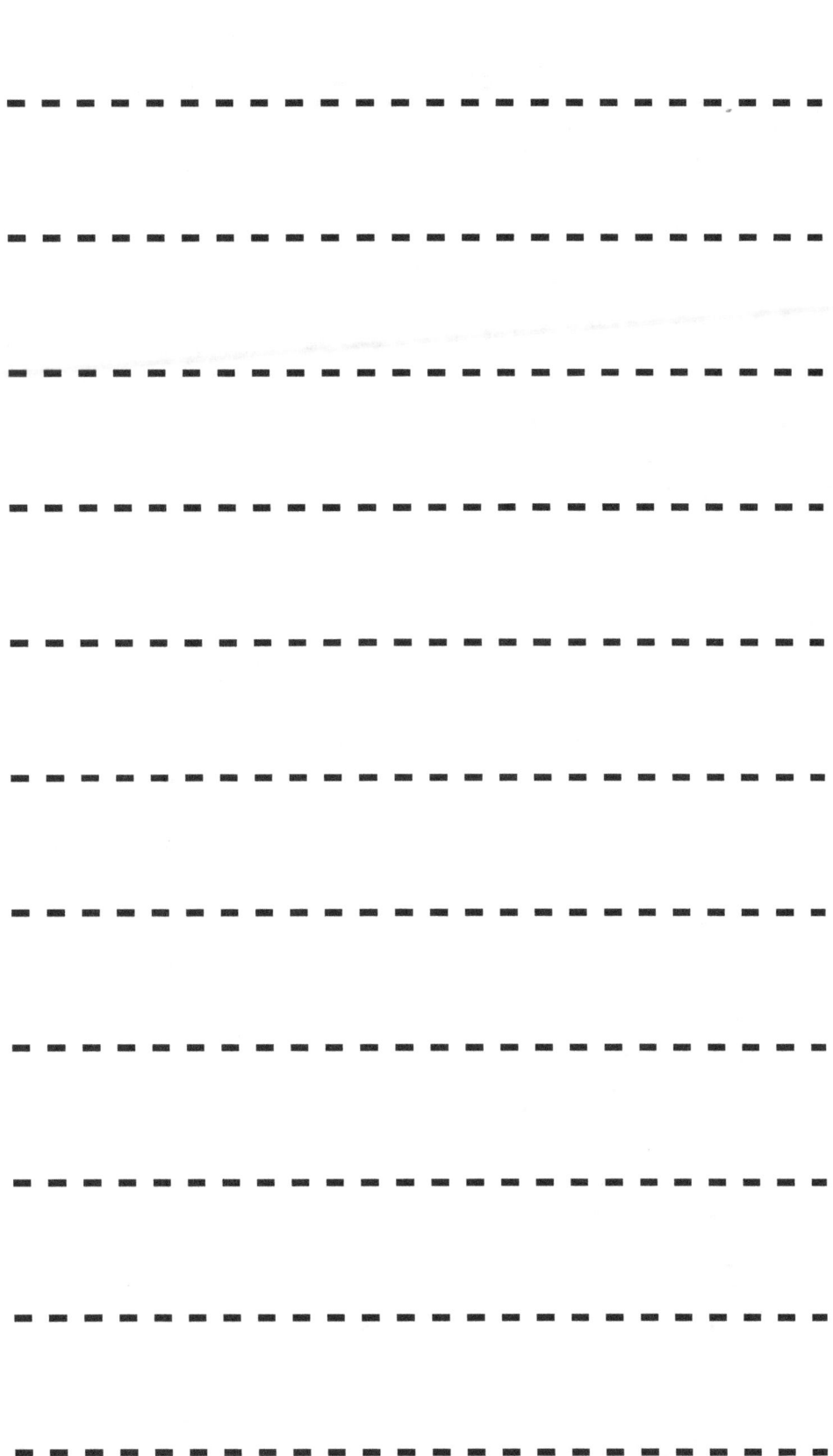

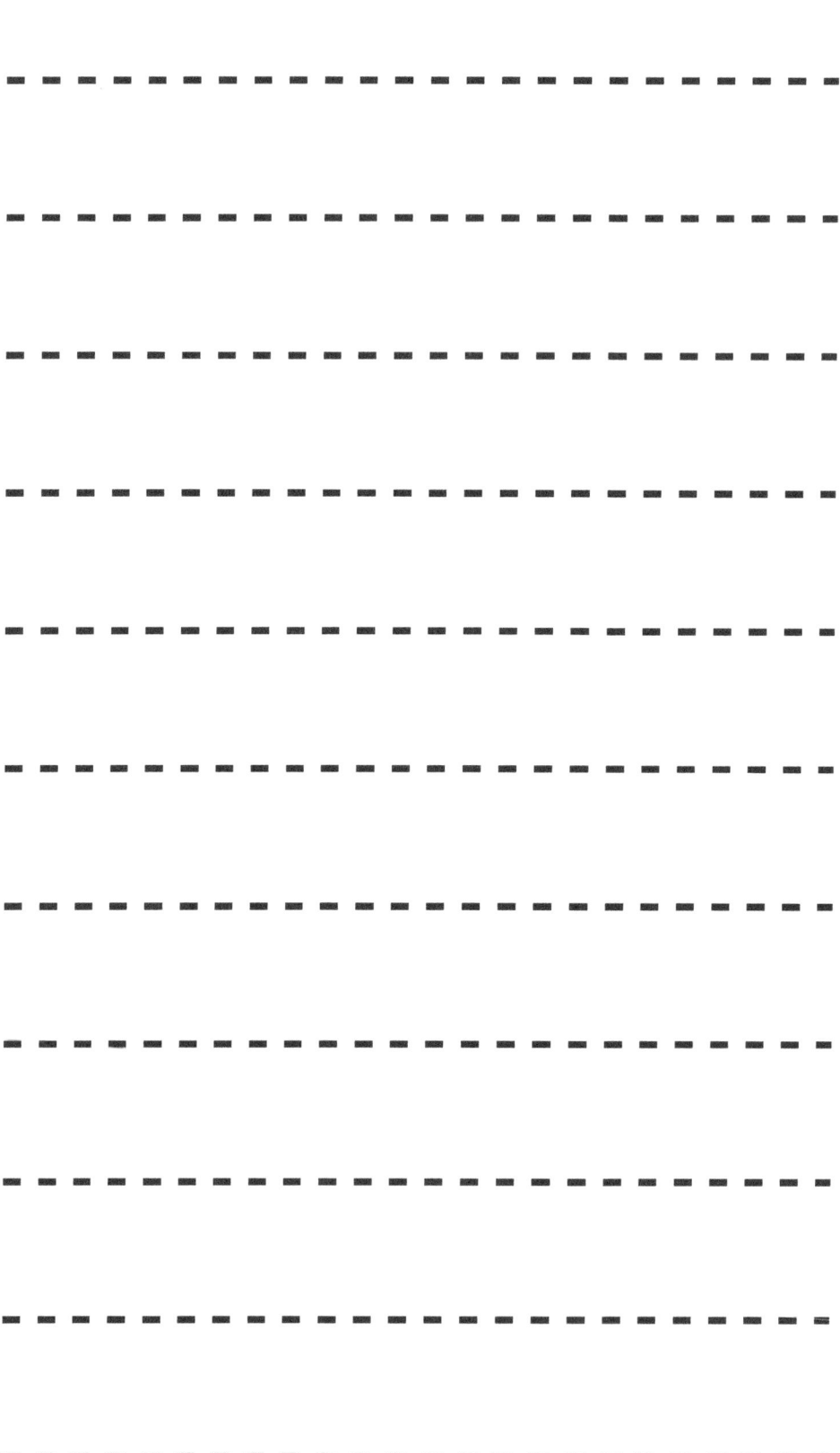

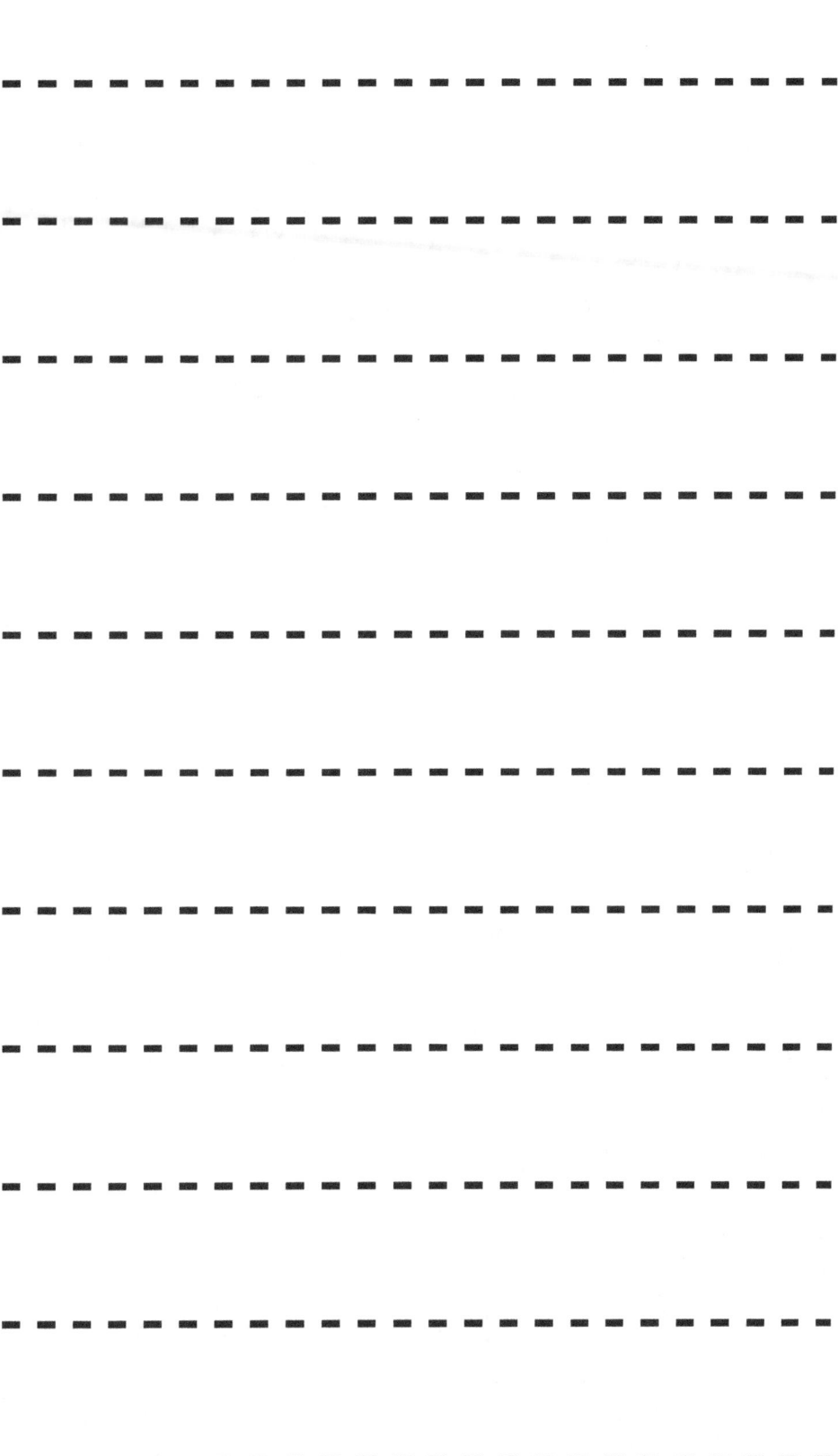

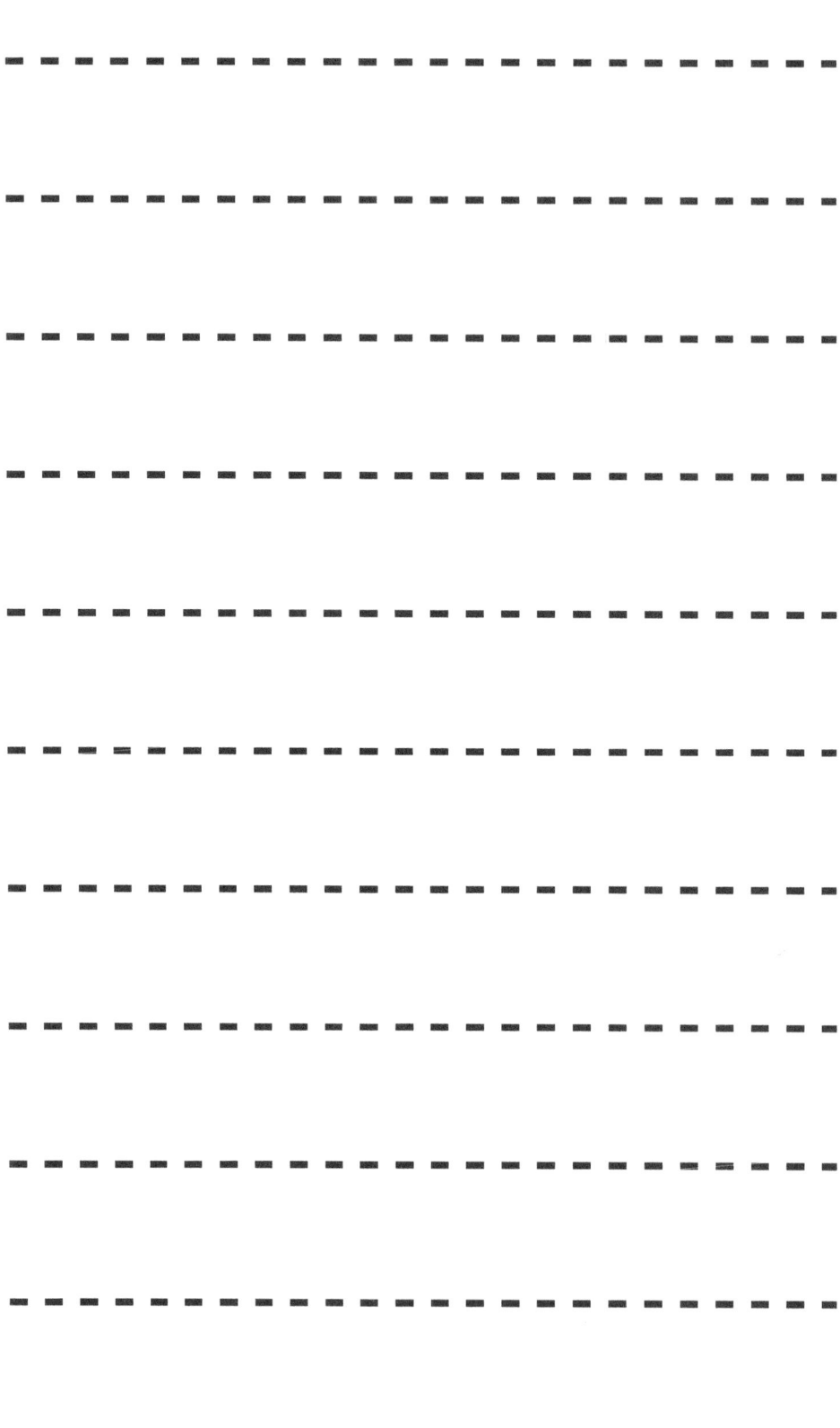

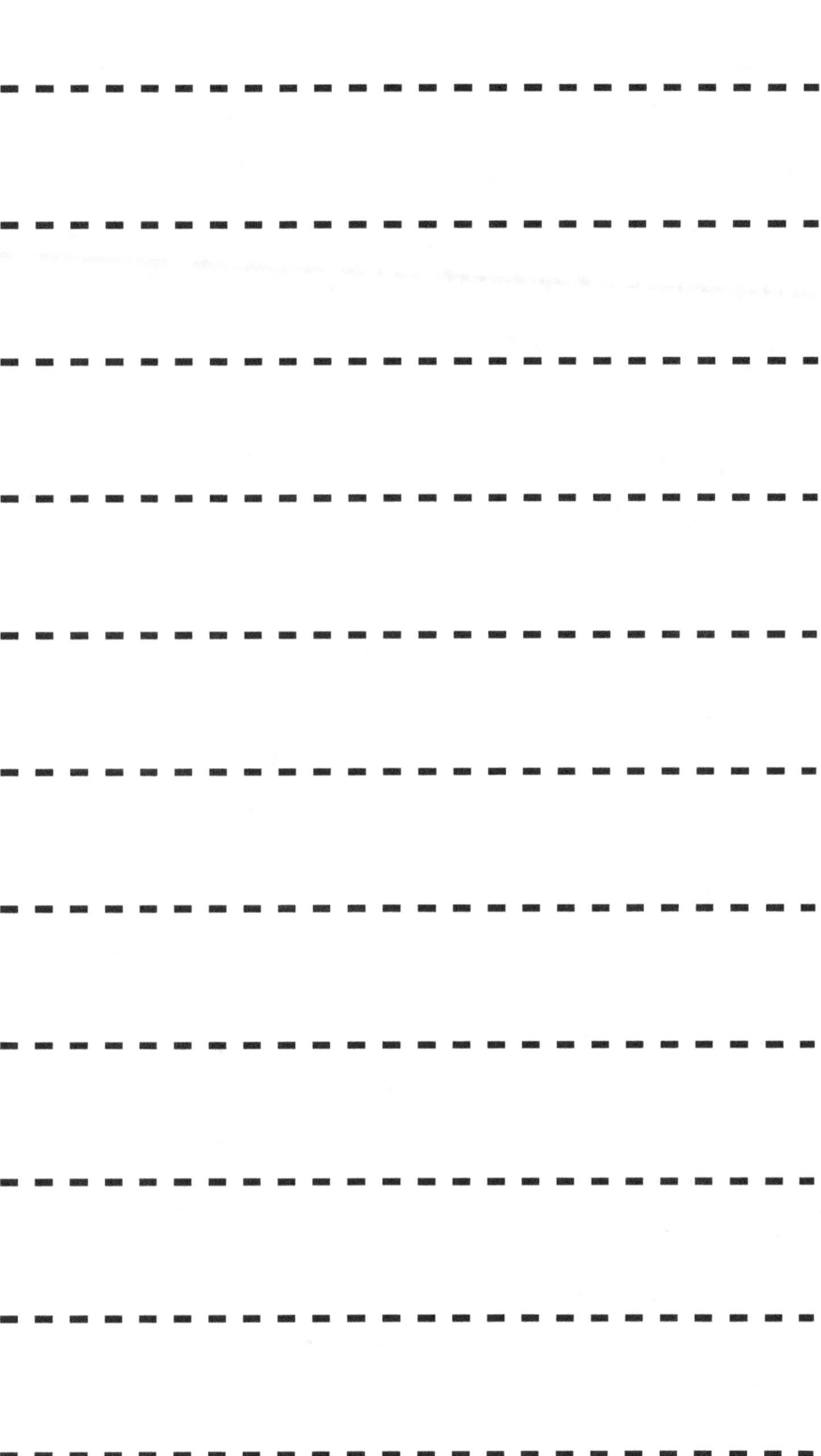

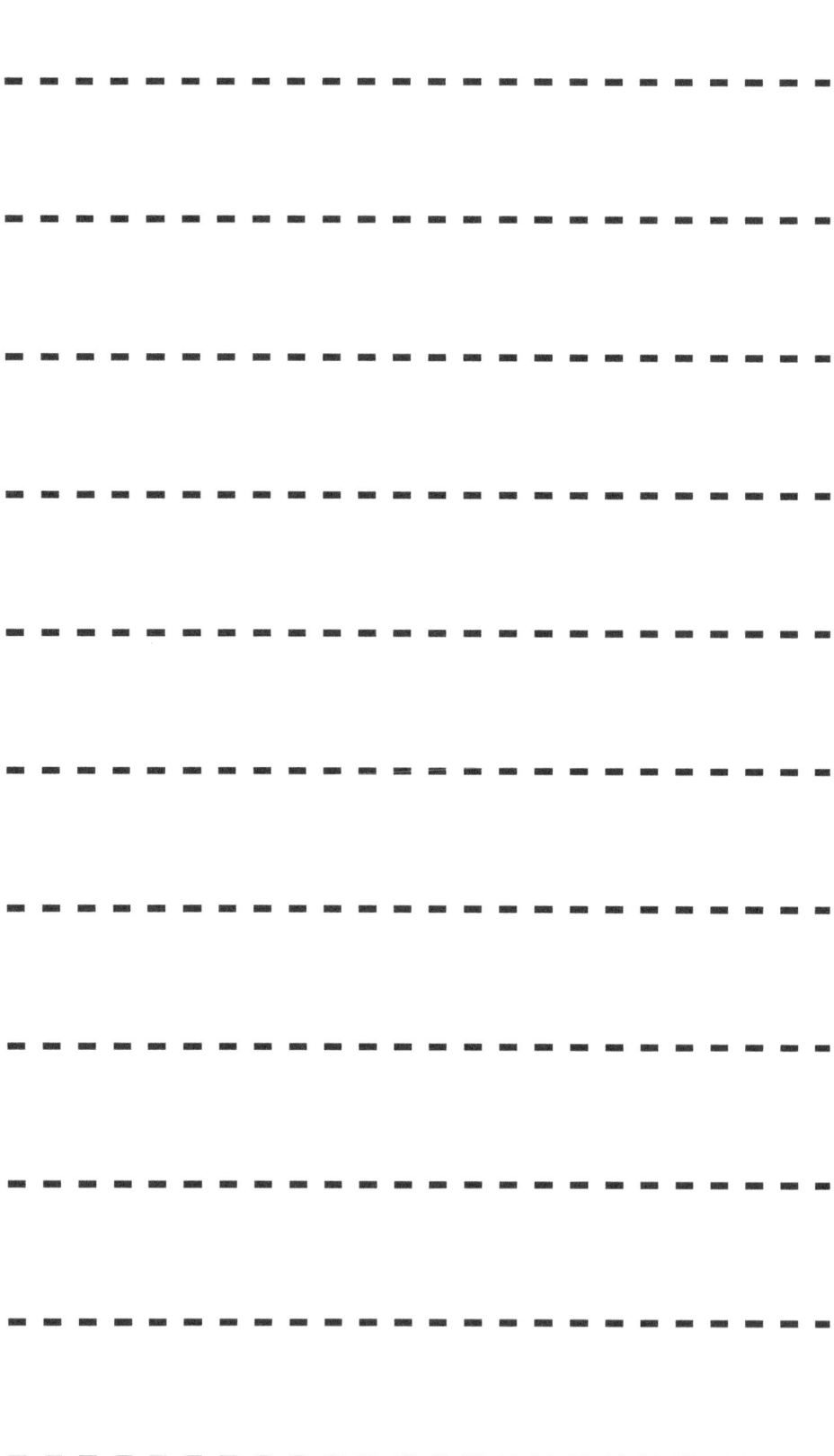

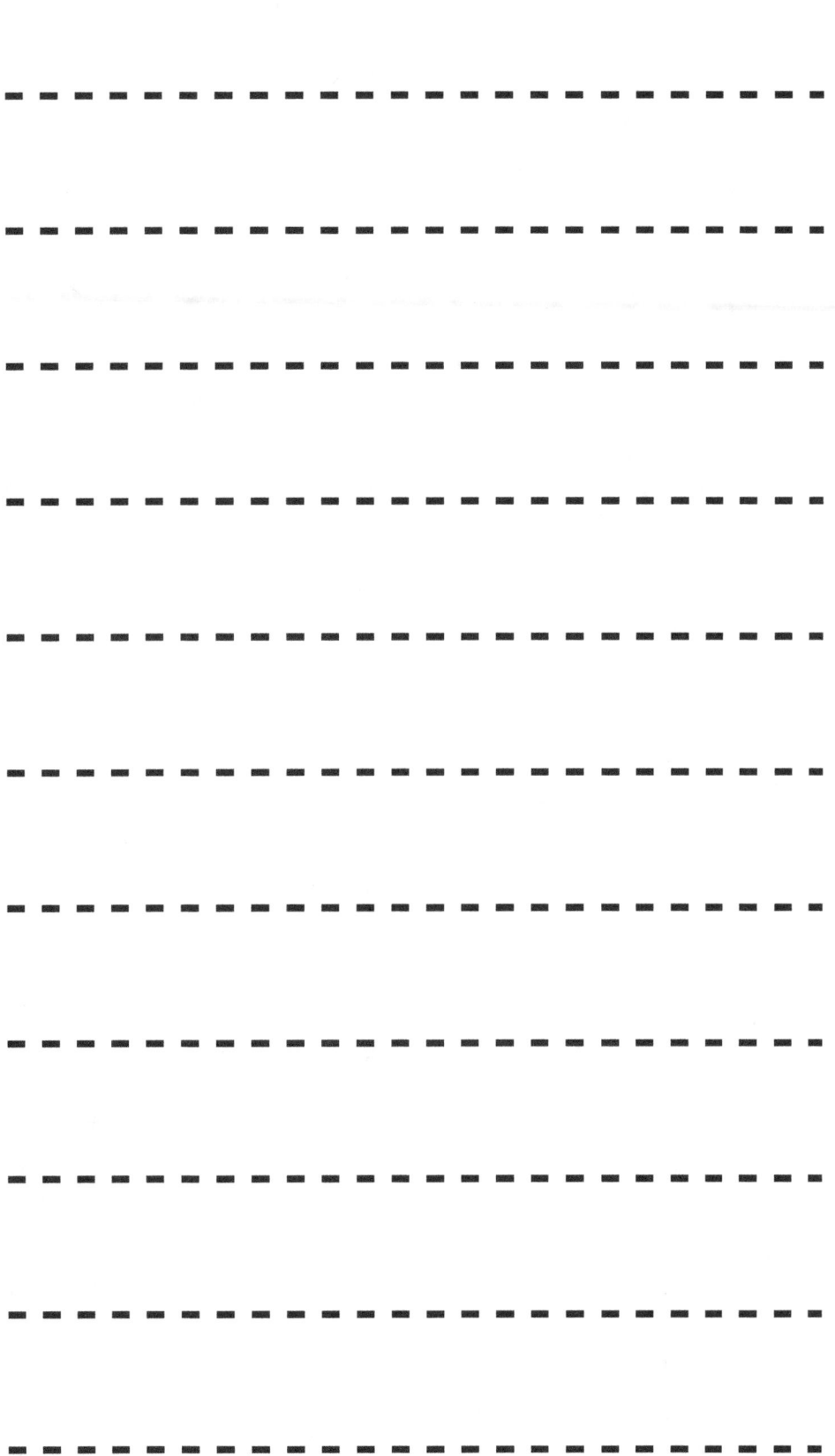

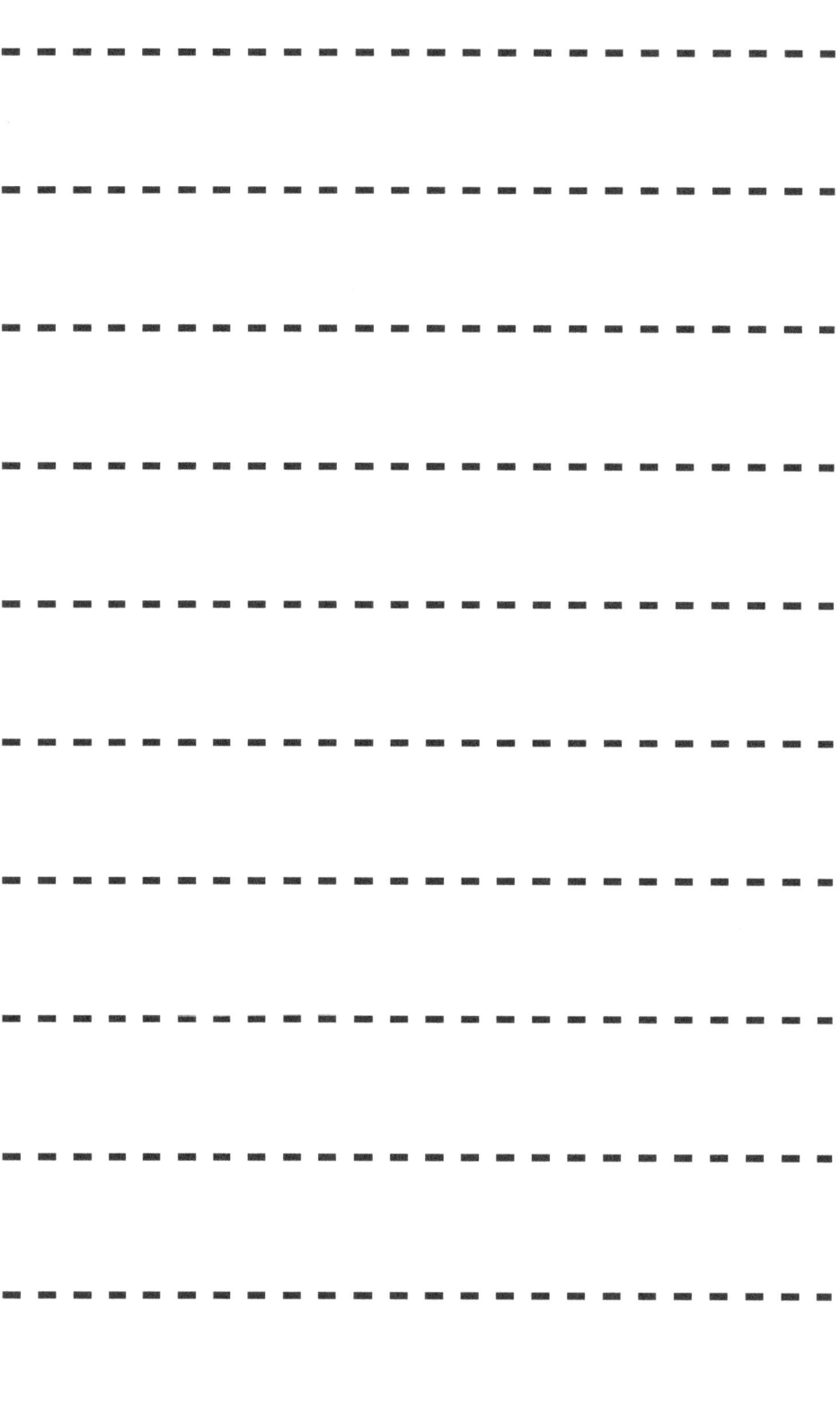

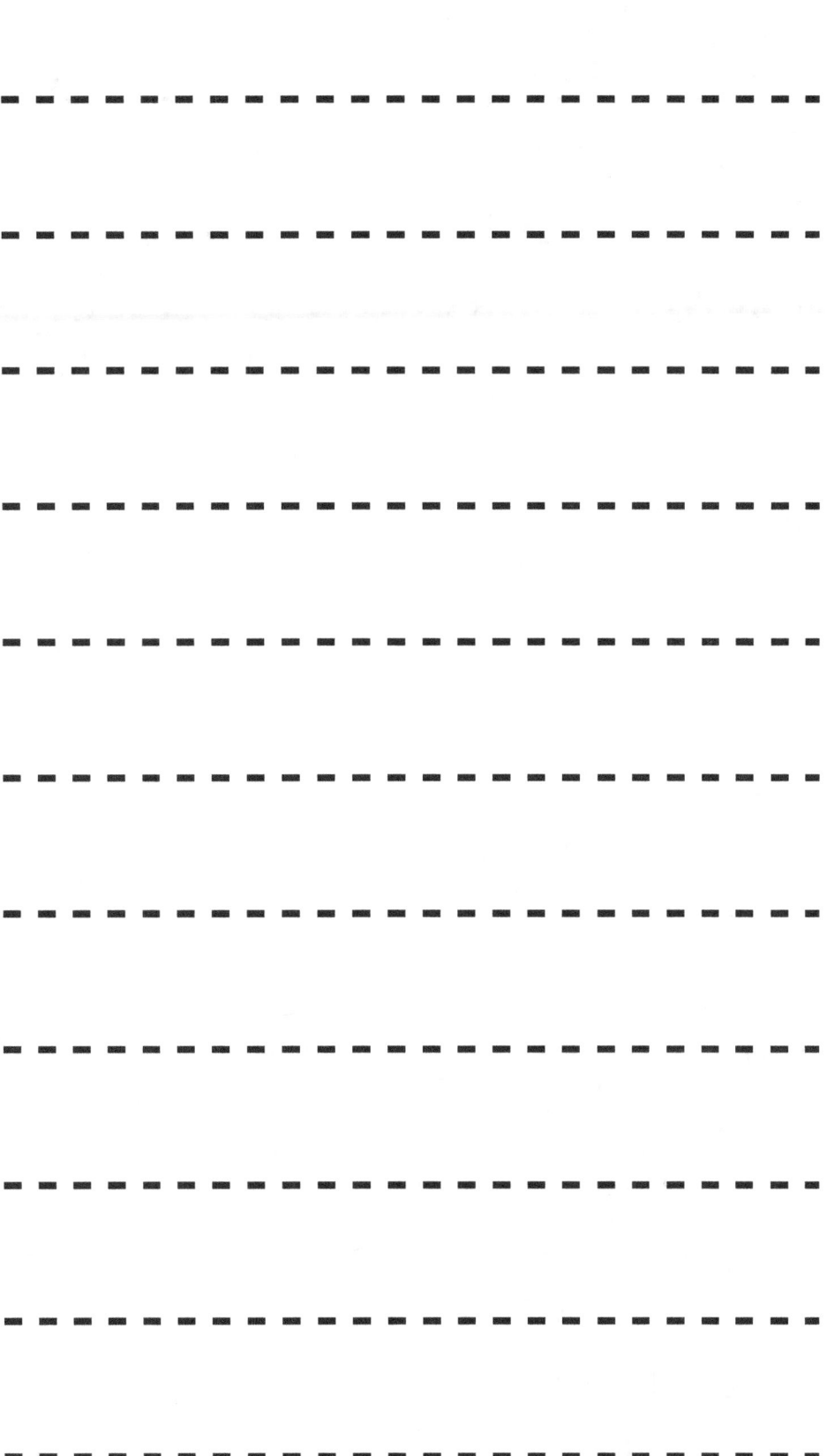

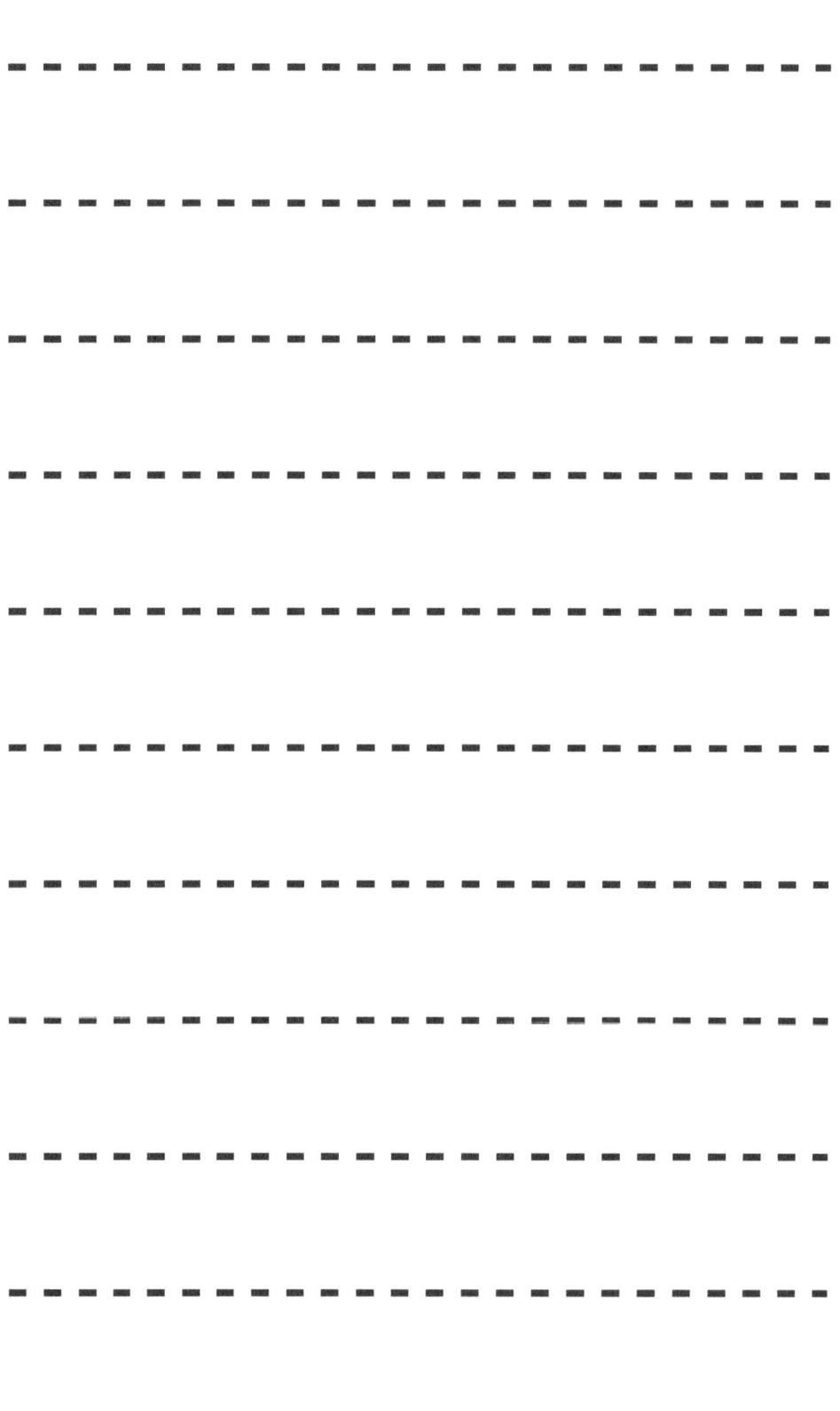

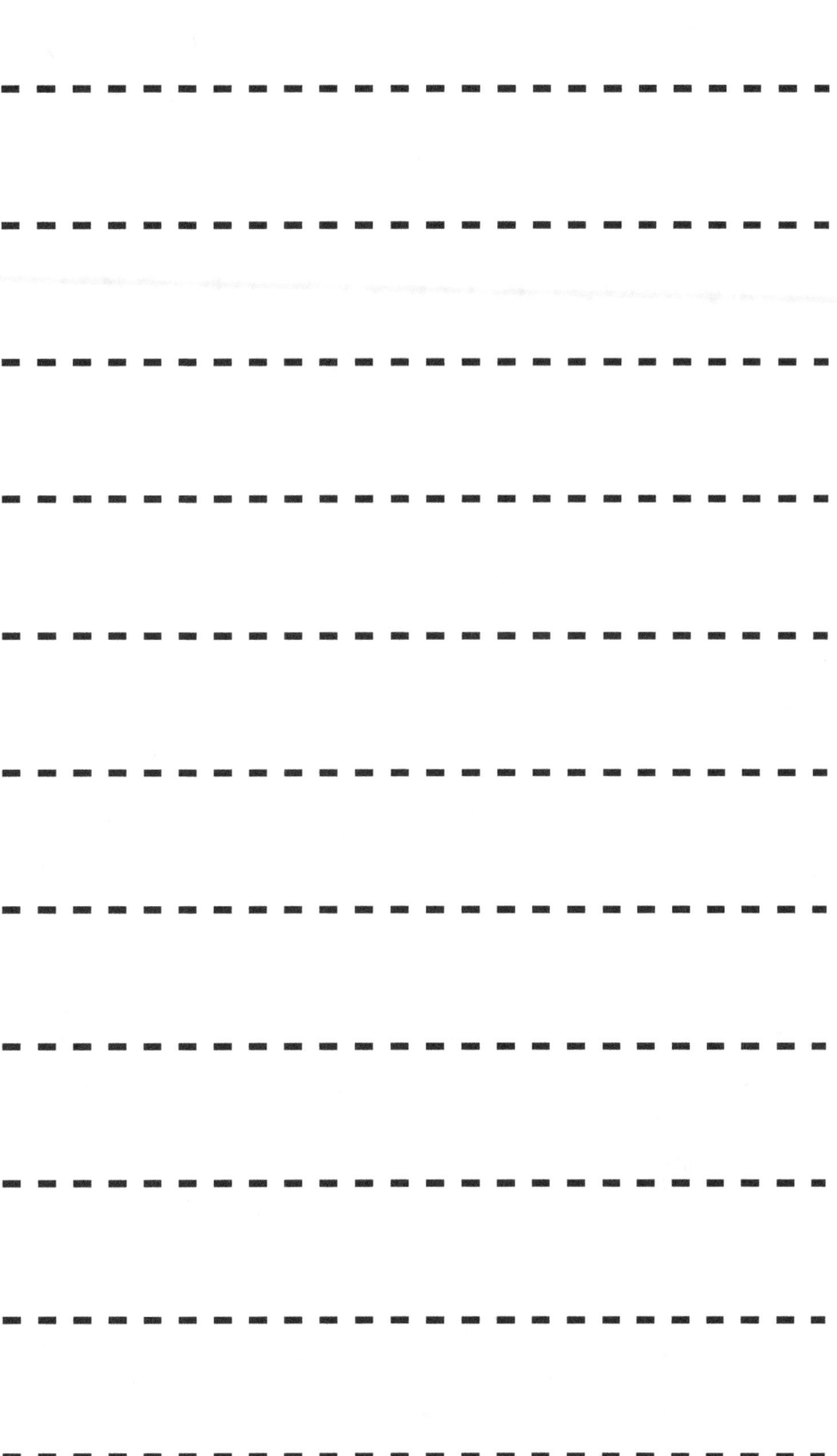

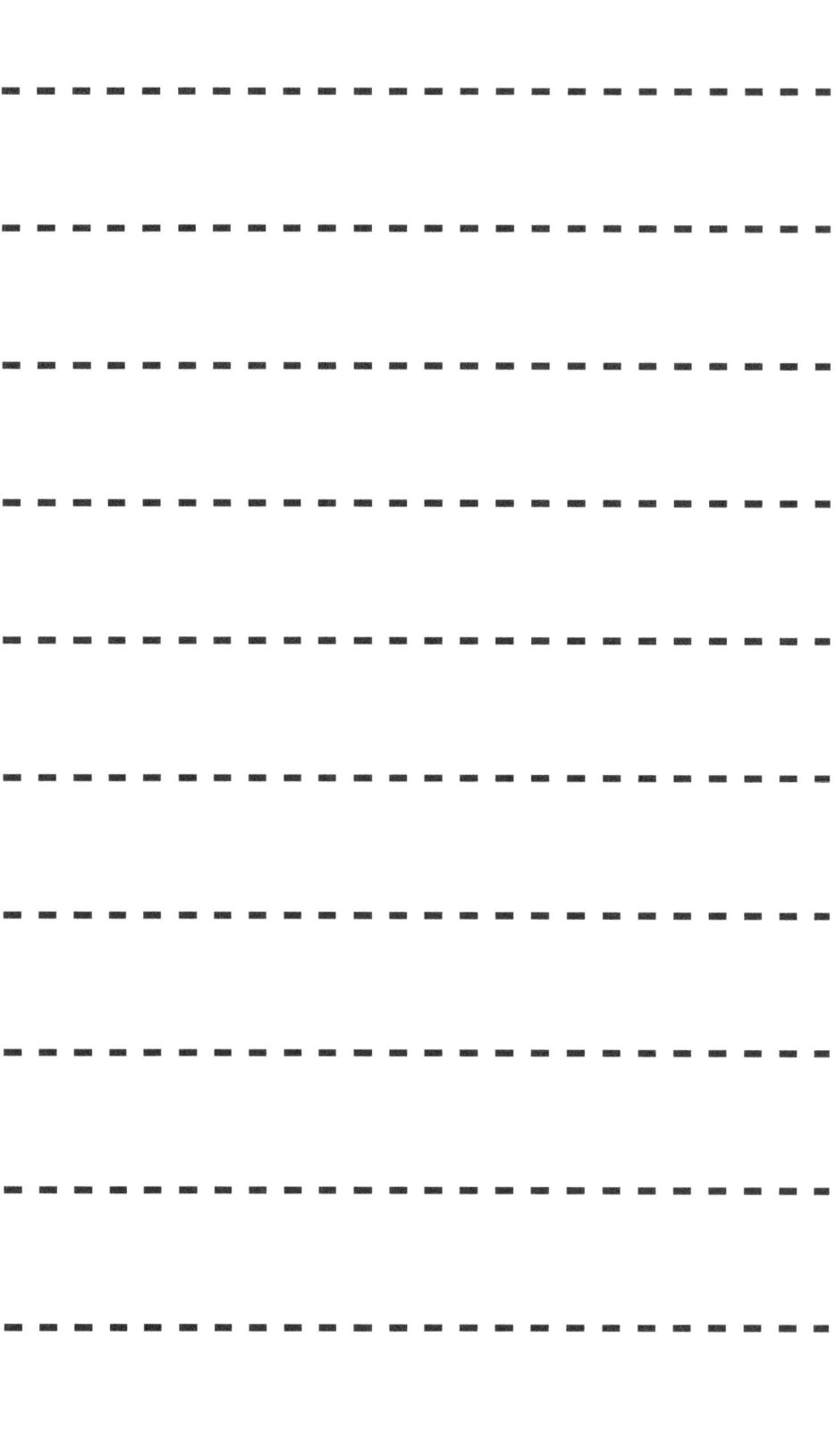

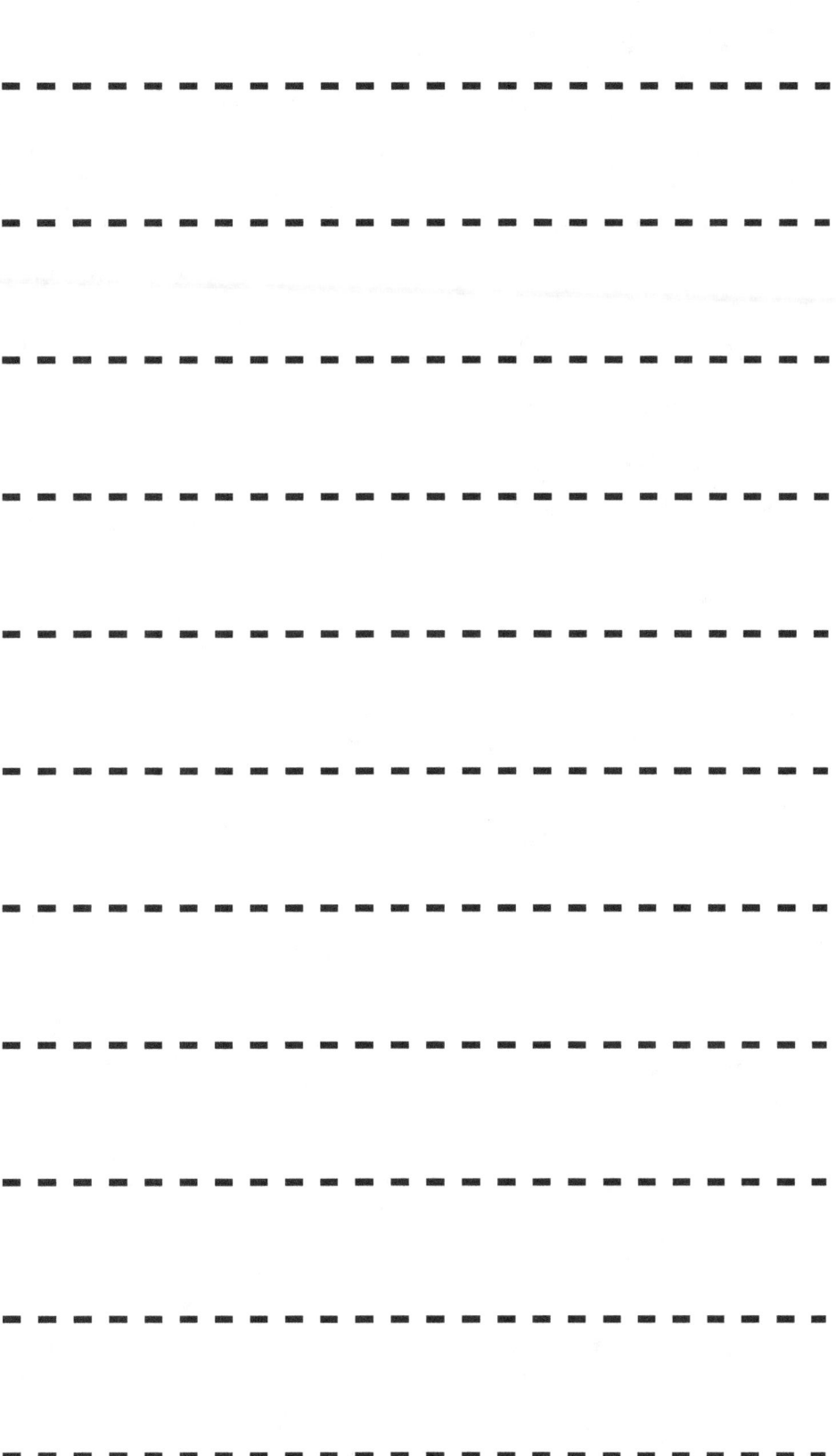

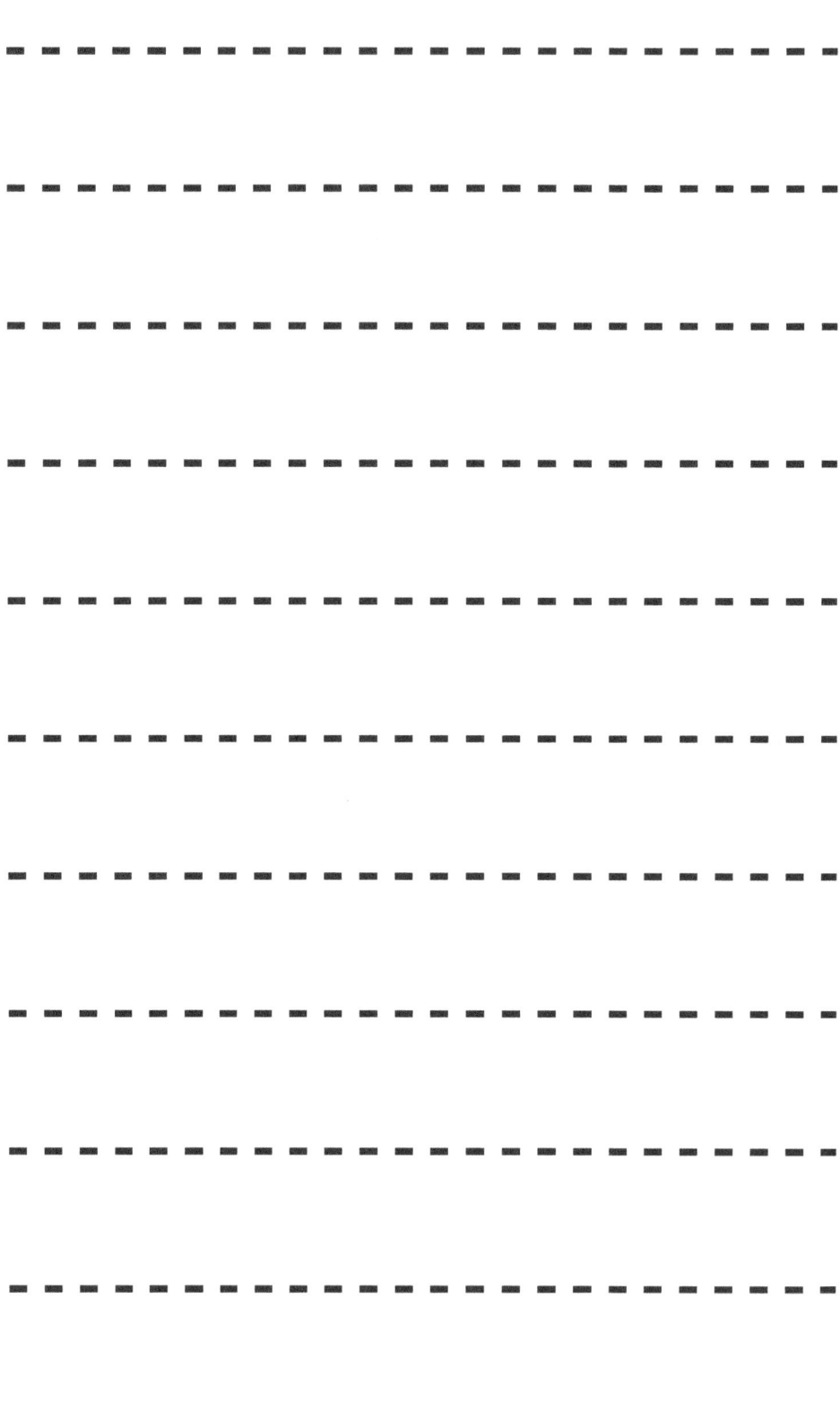

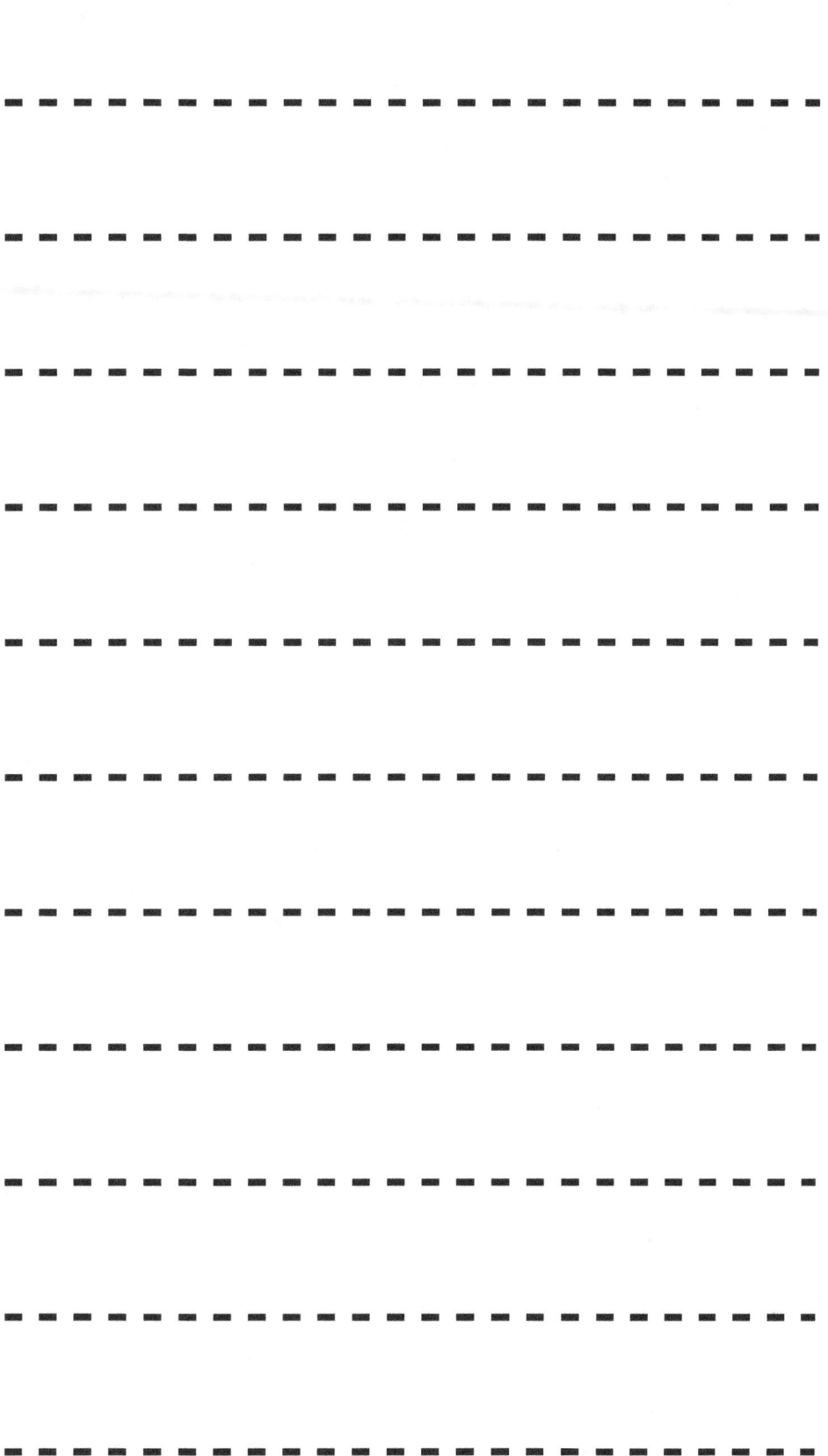

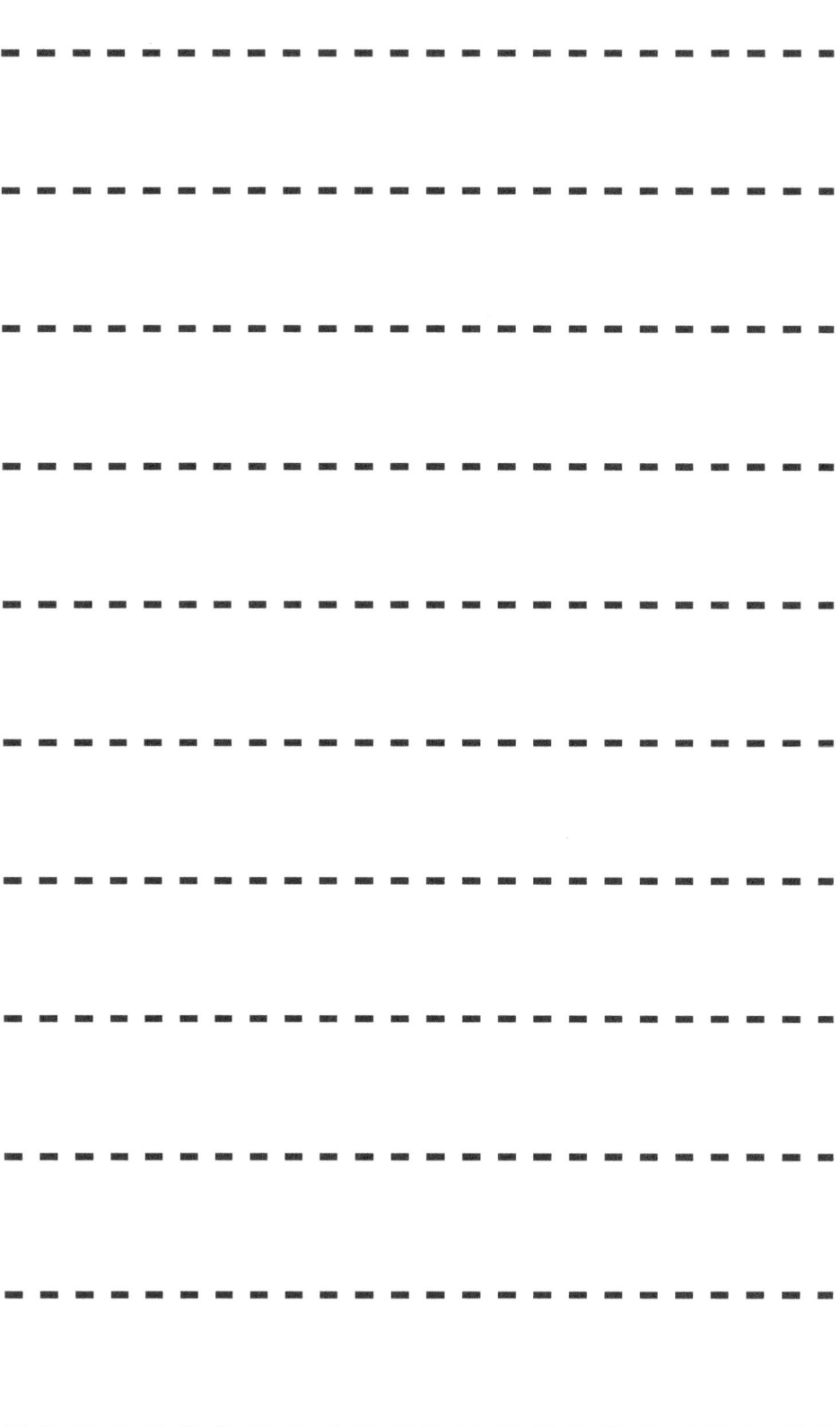

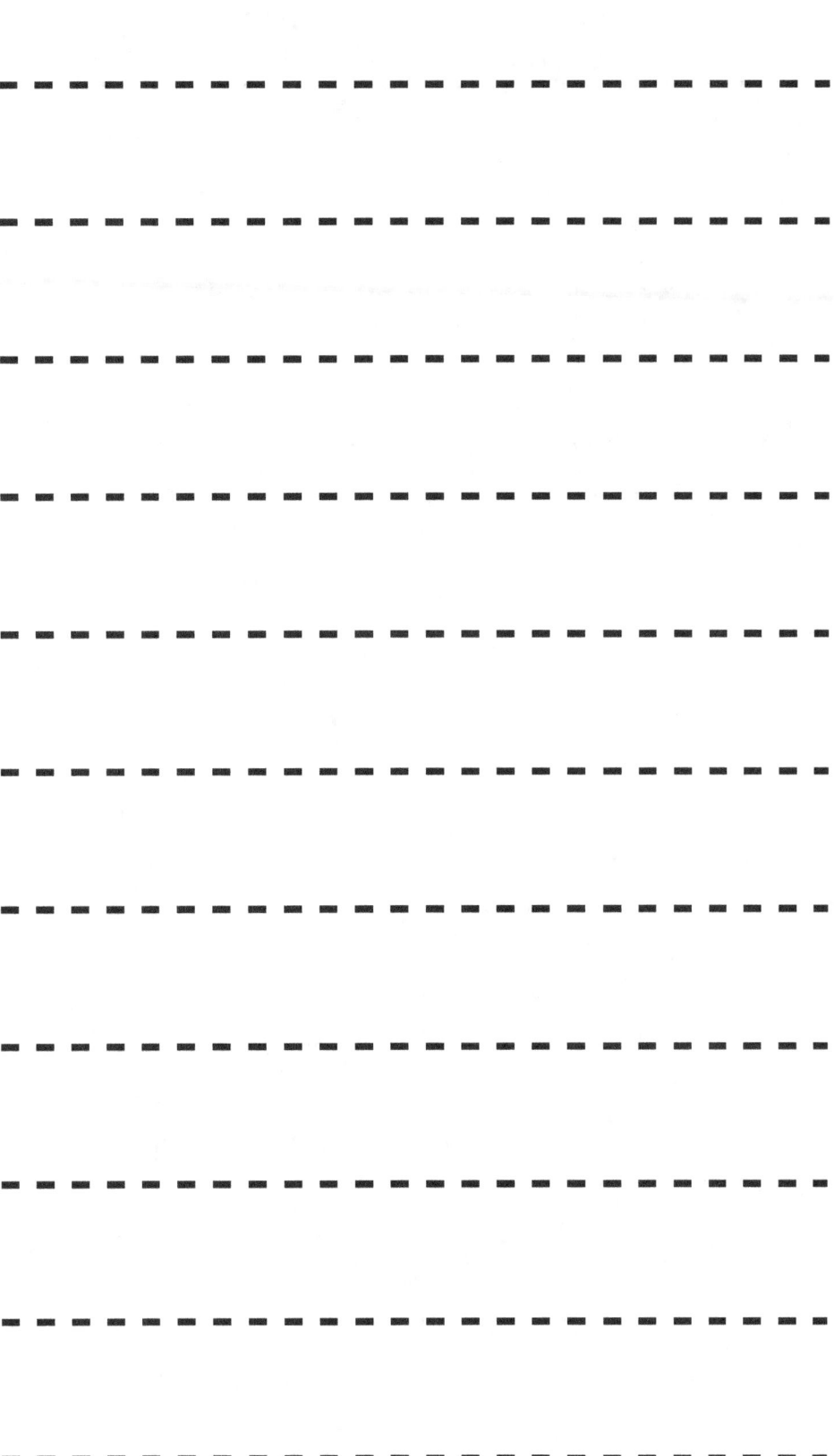

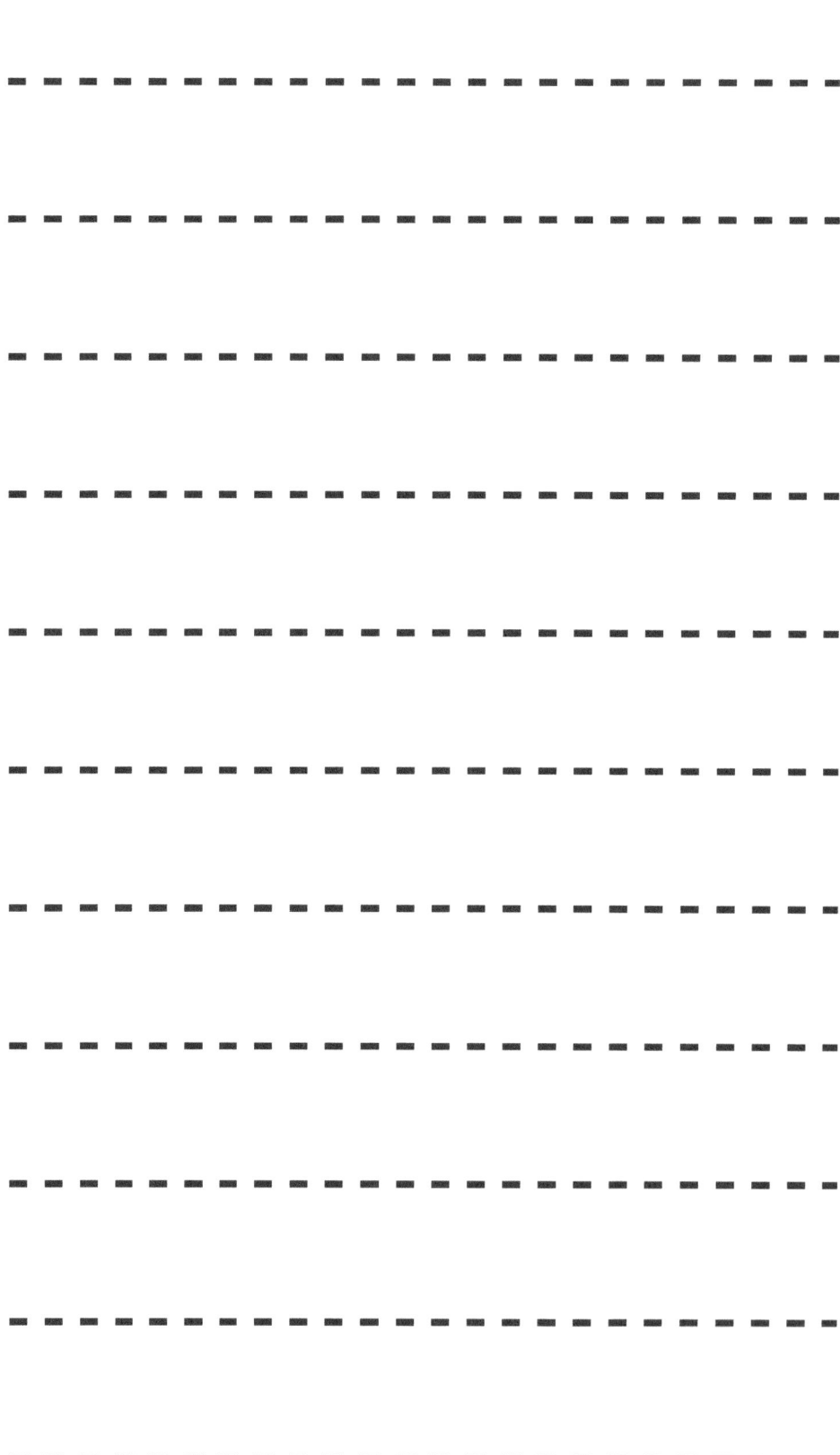

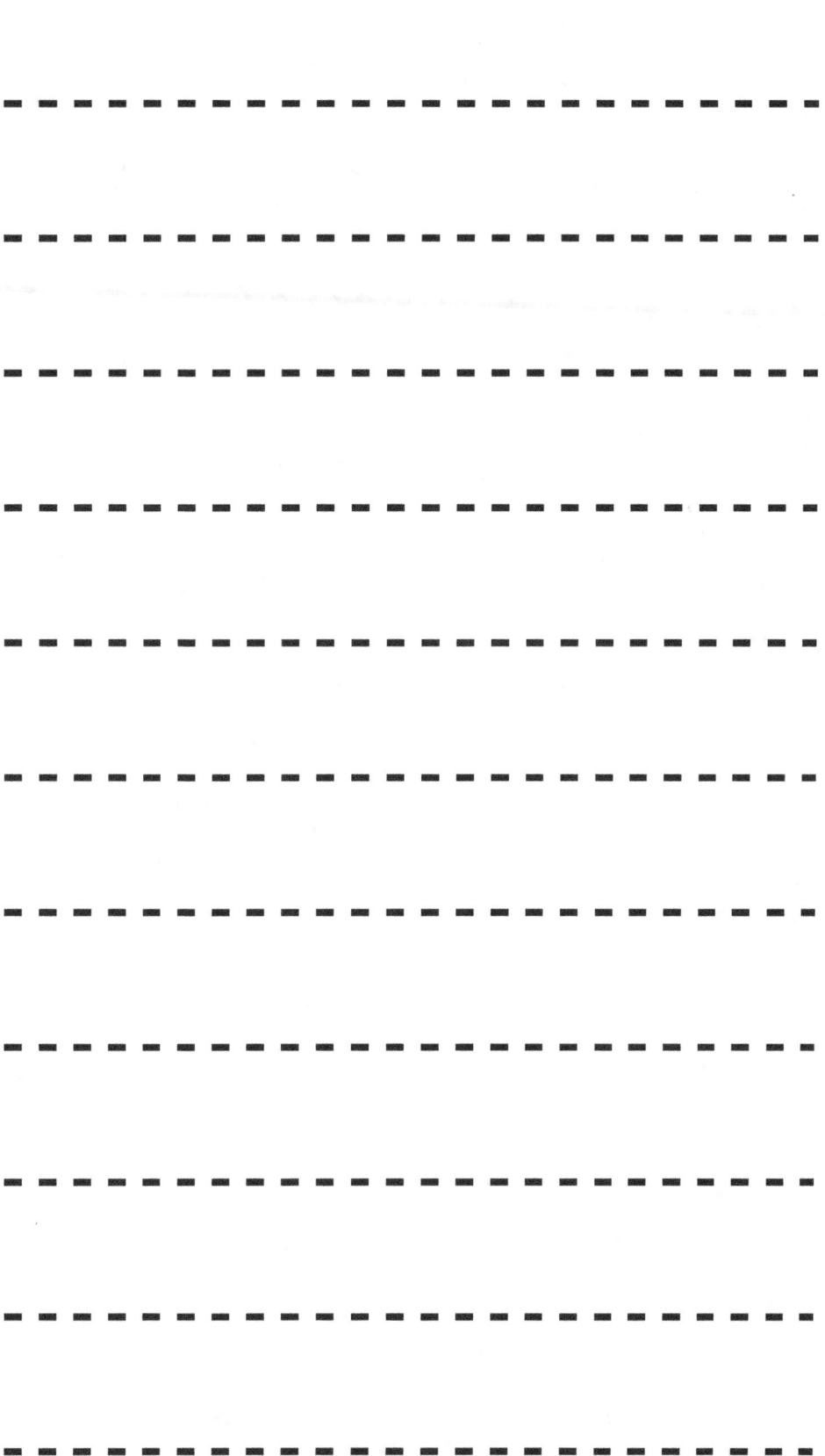

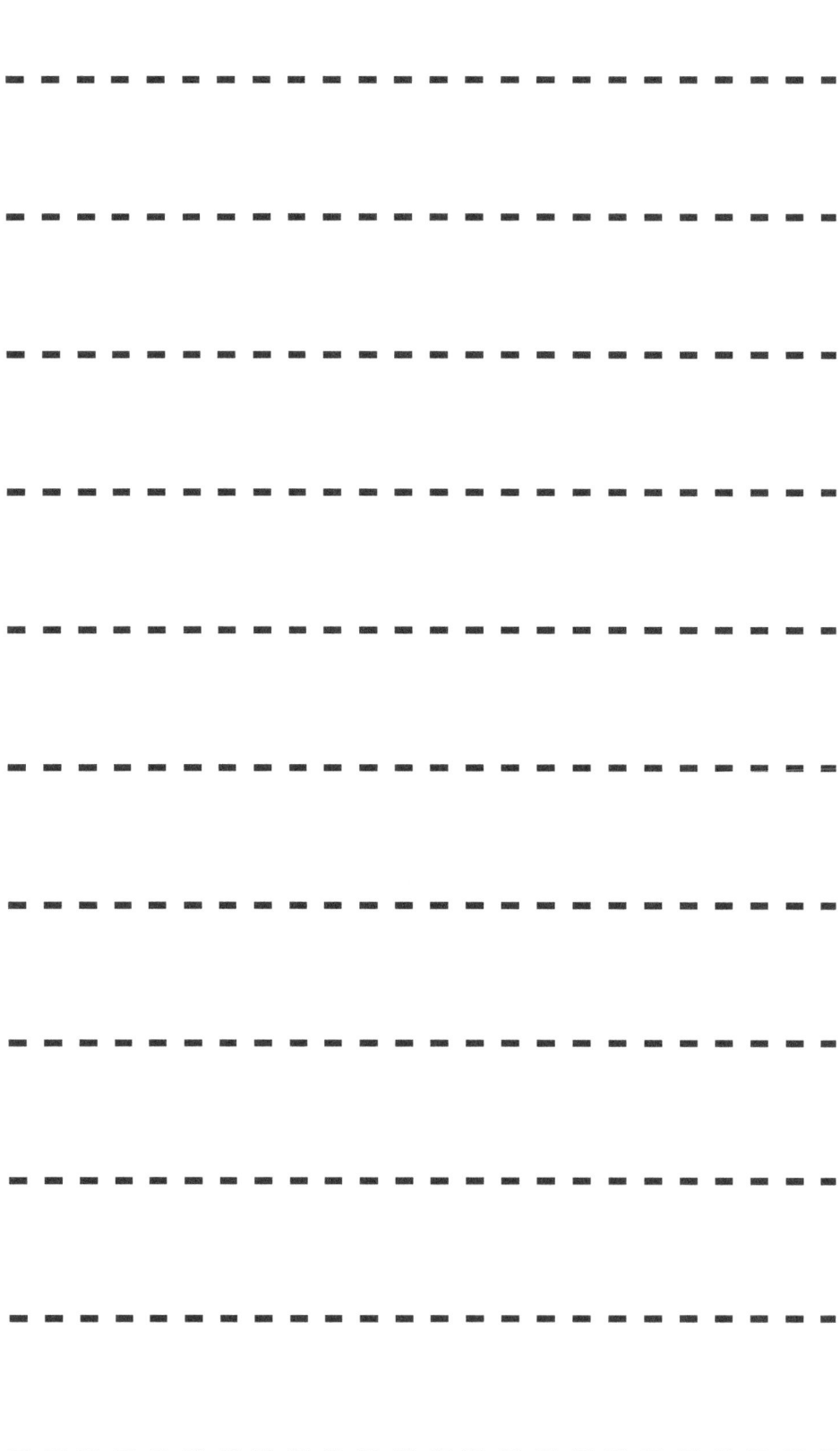

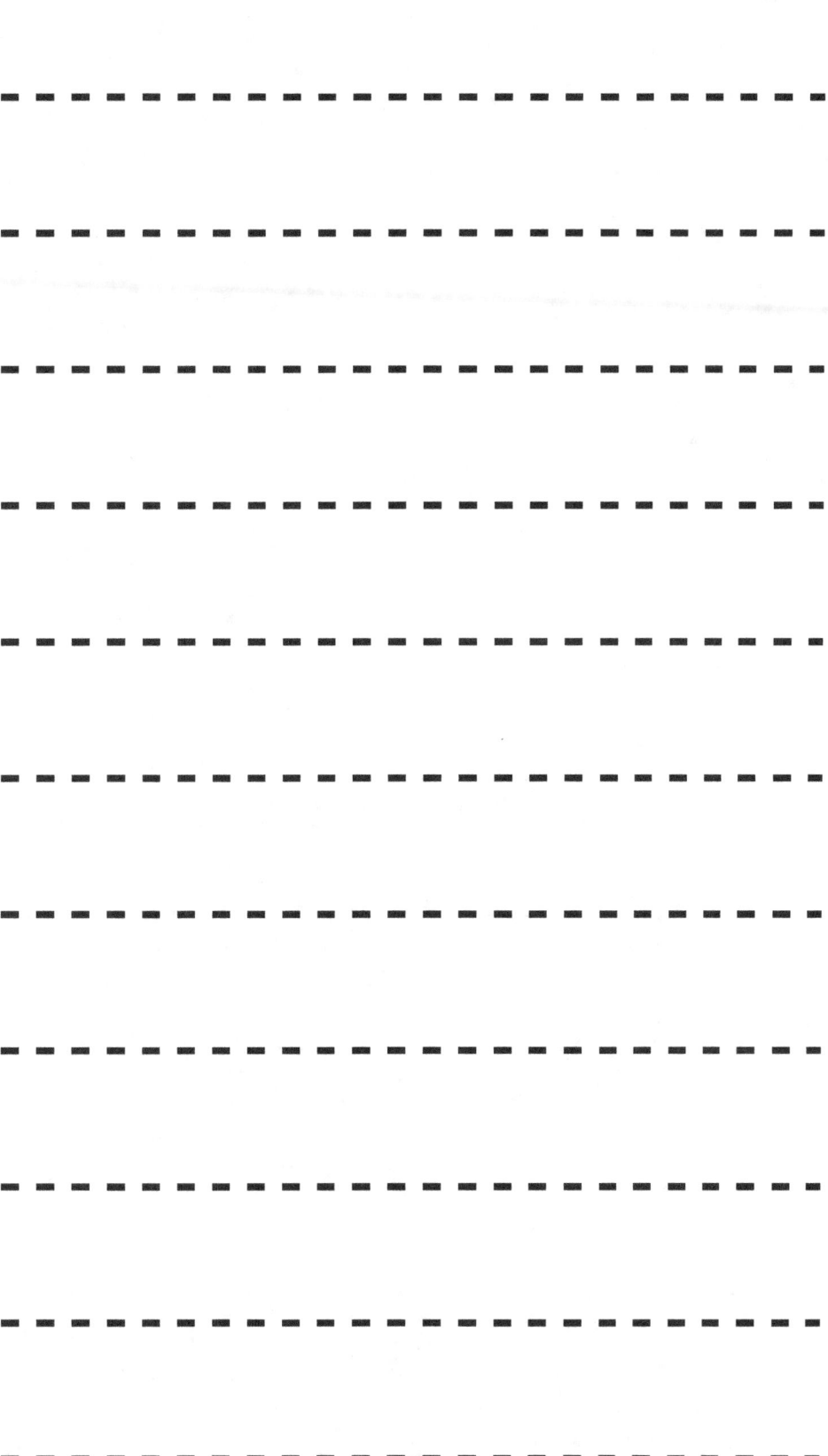

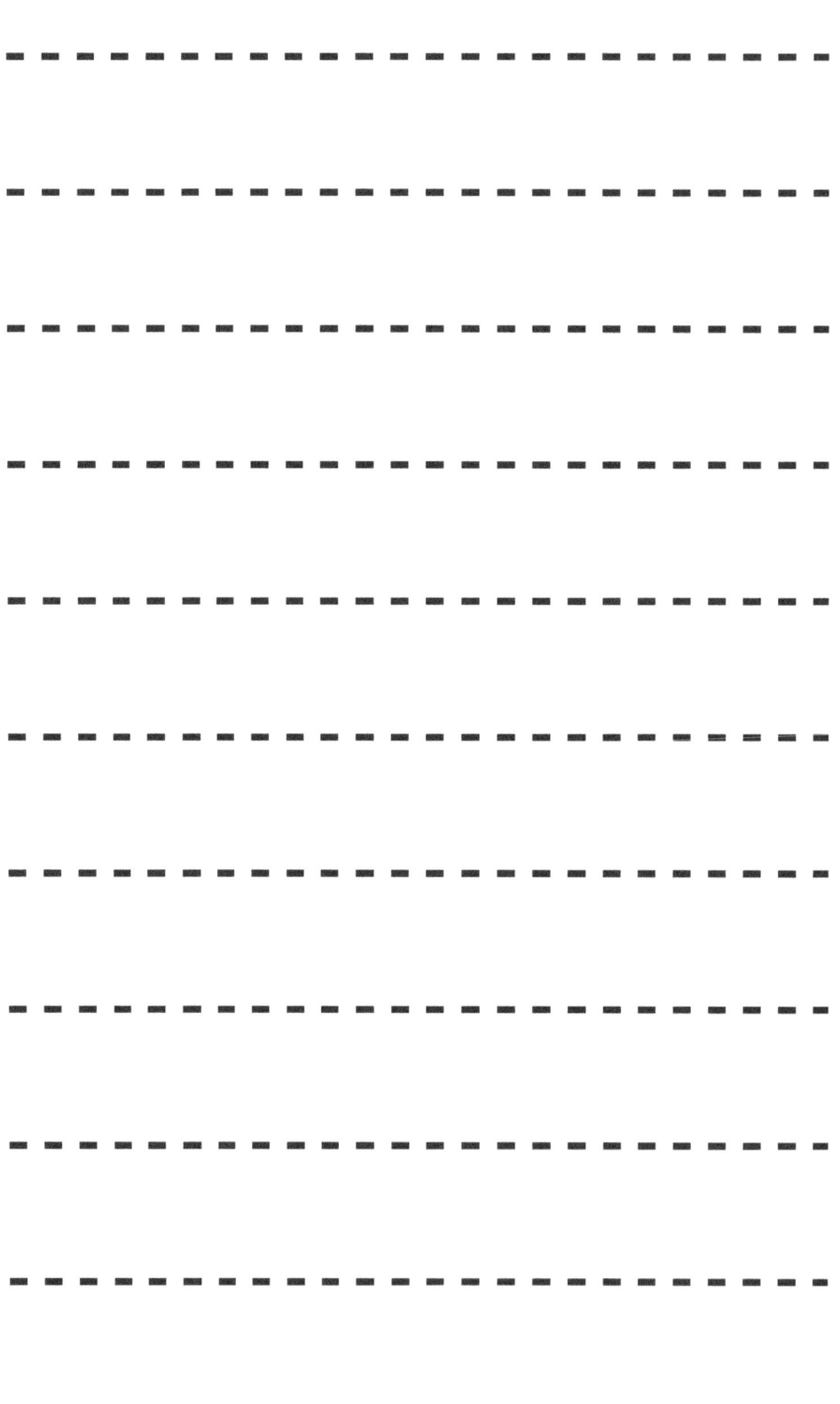

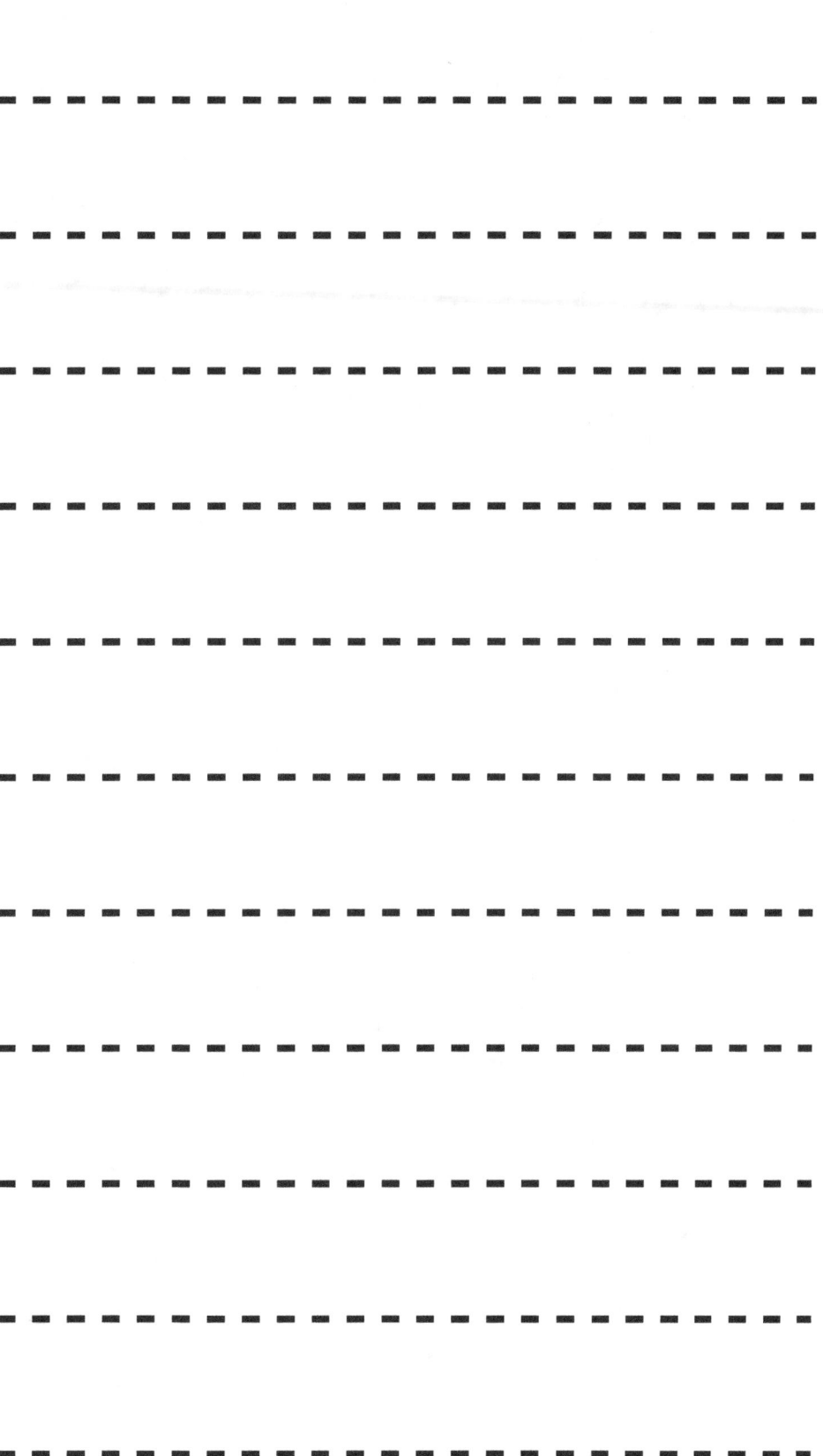

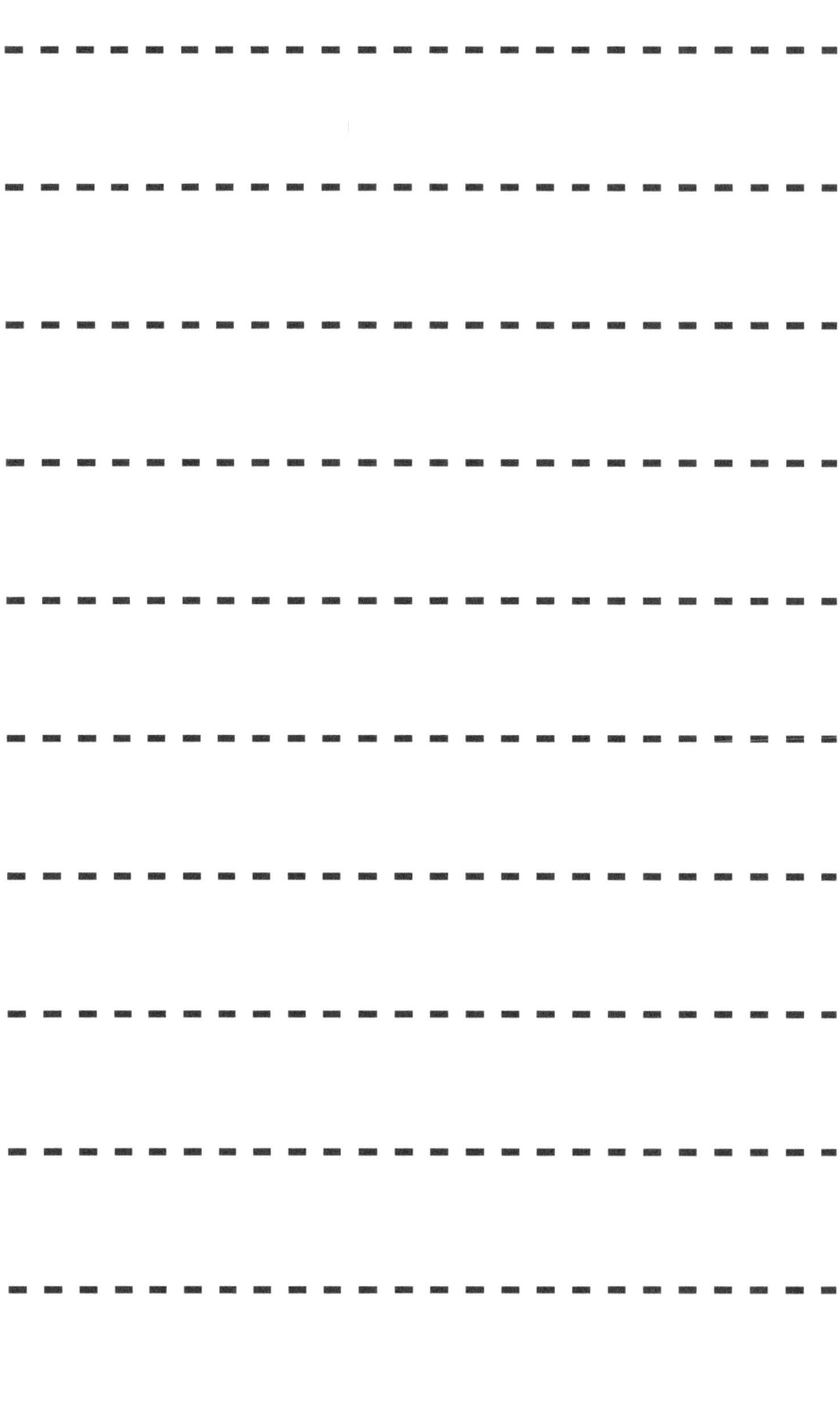

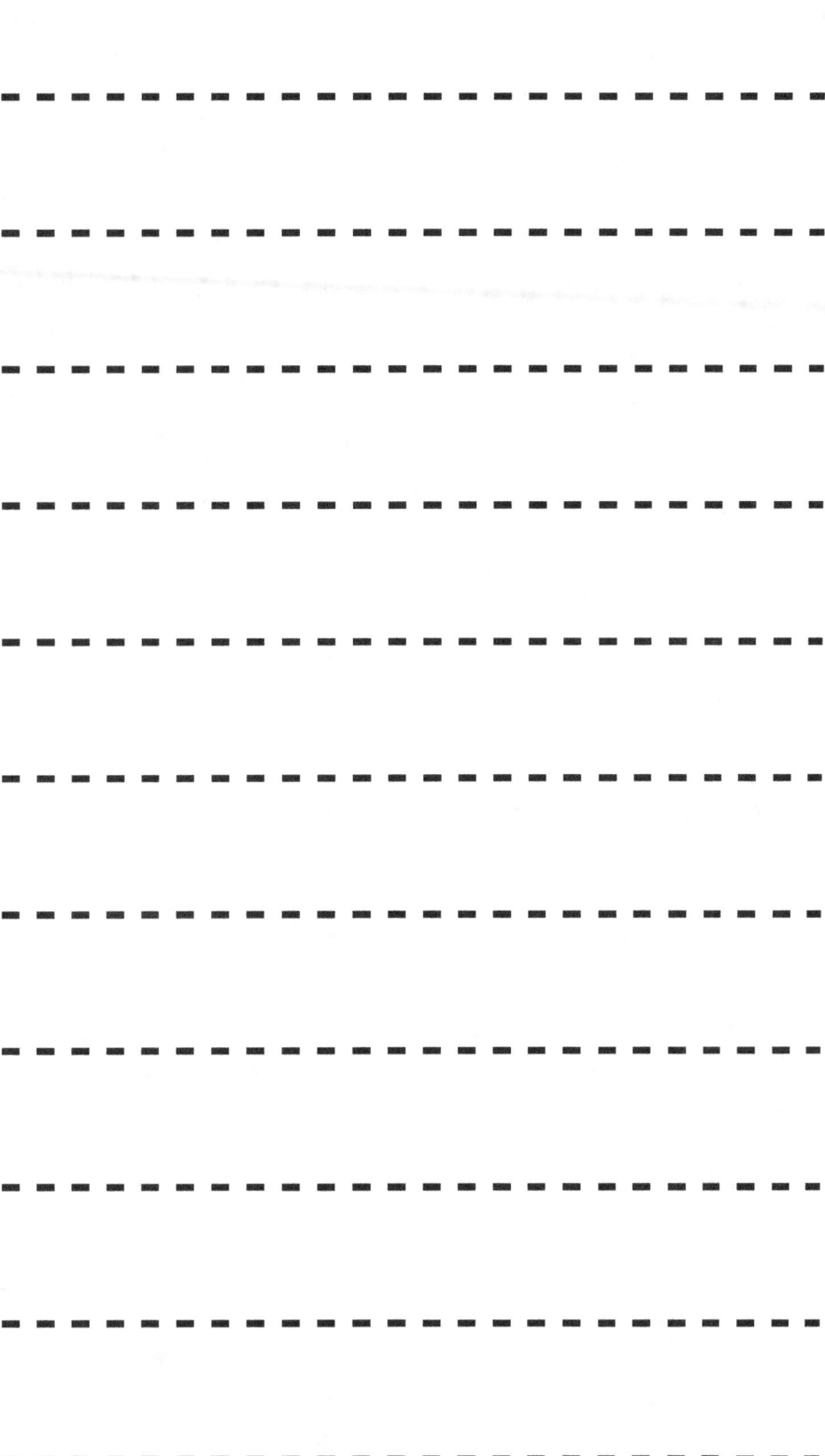

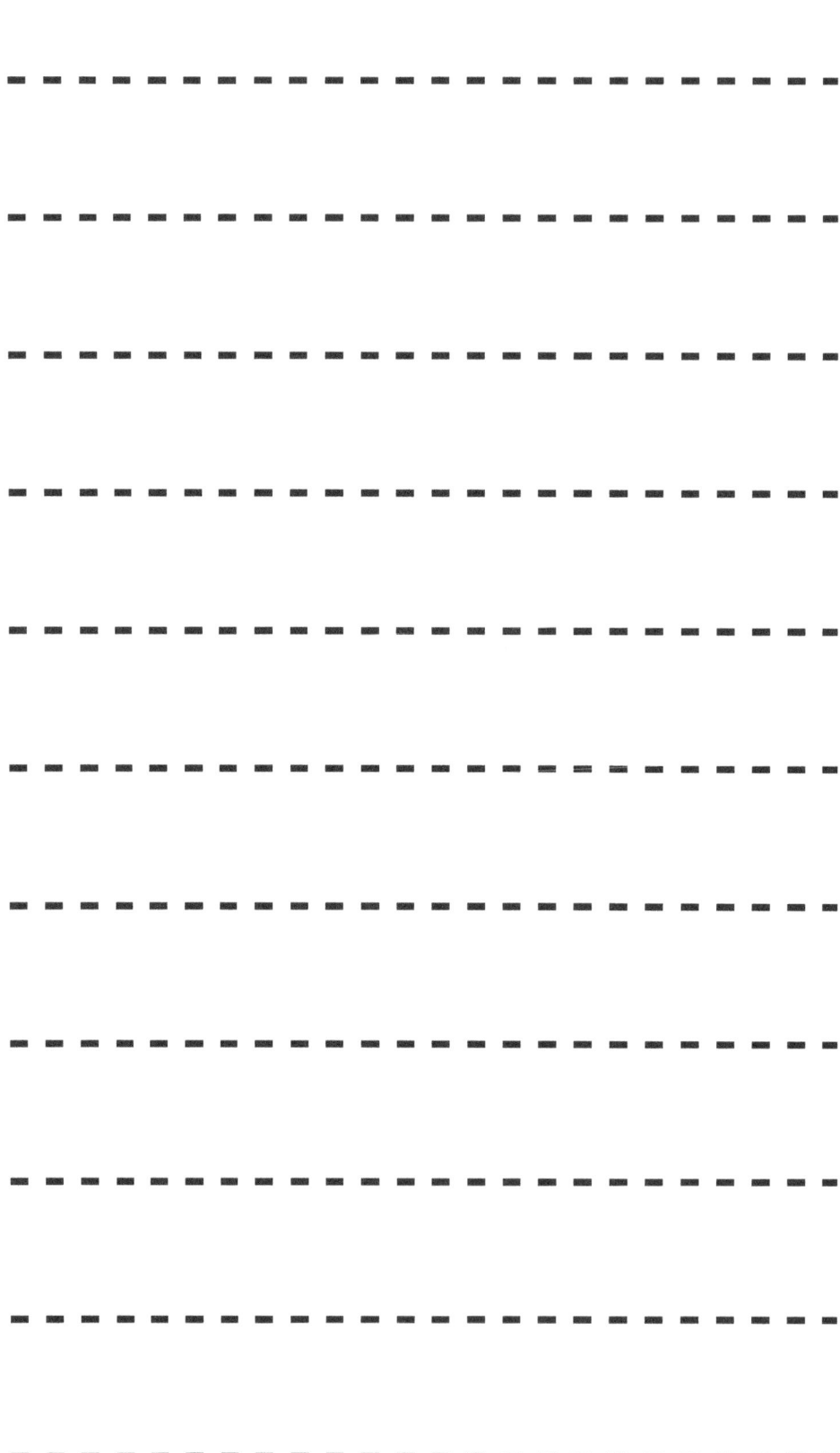

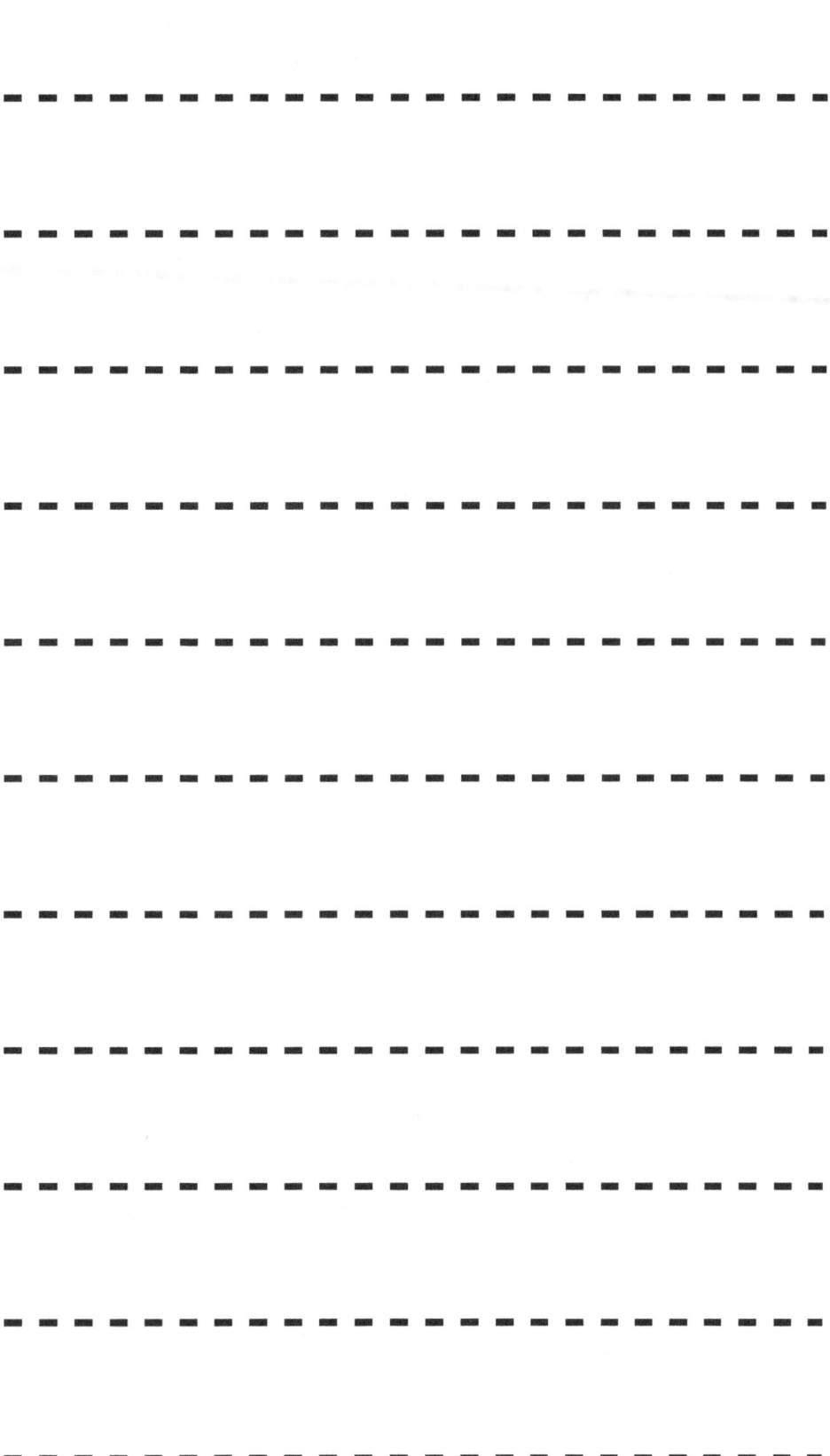

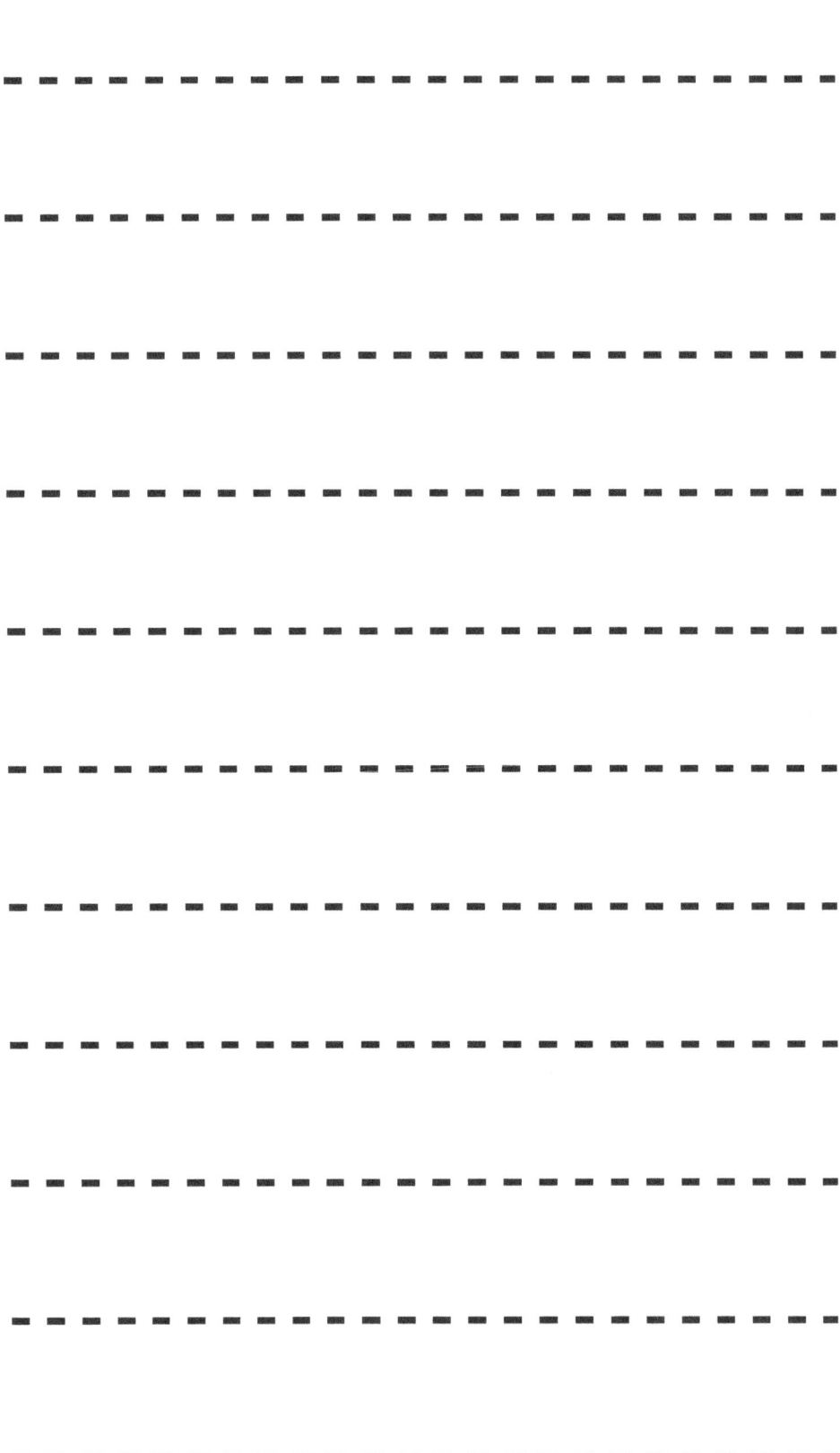

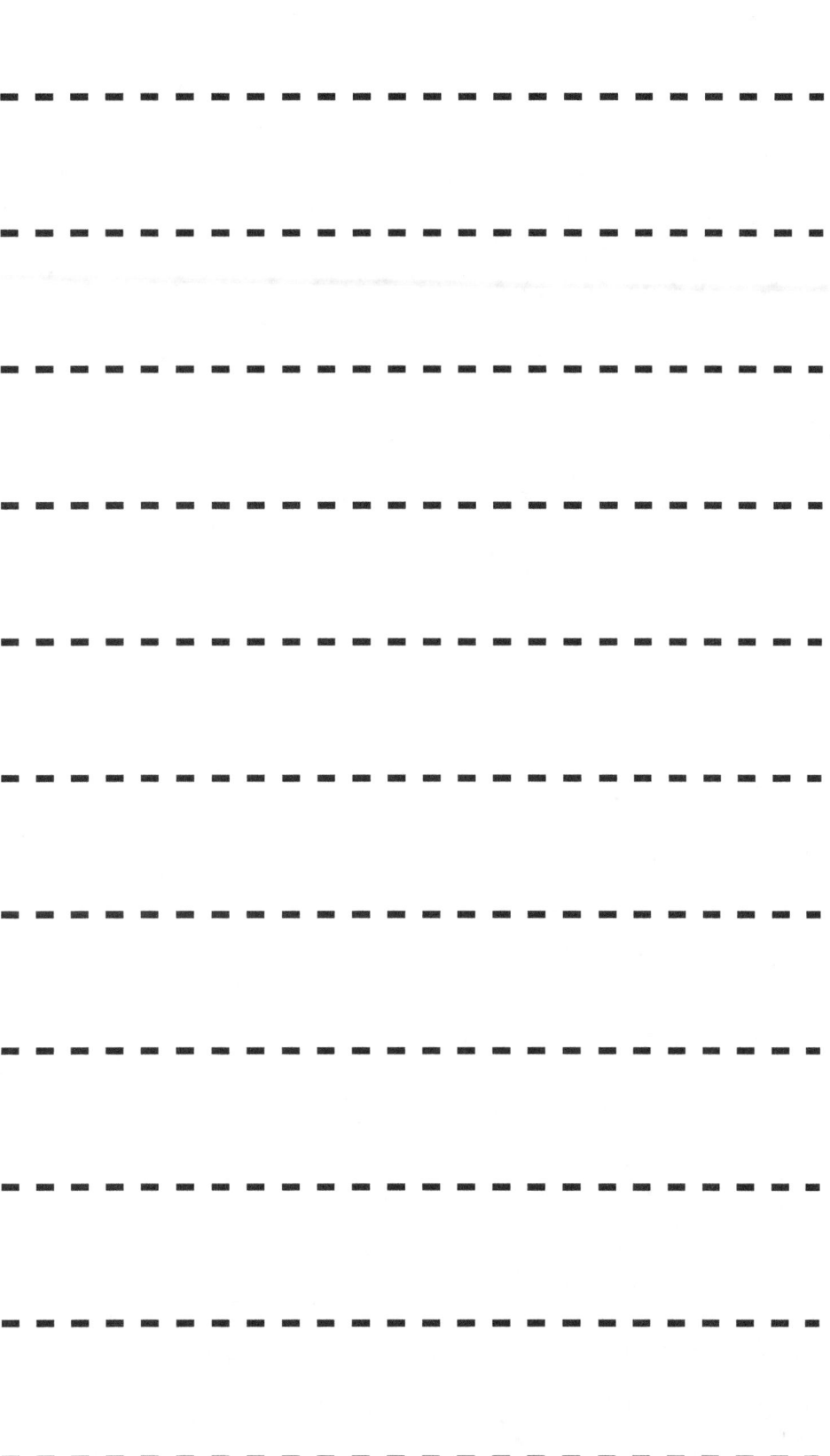

www.ingramcontent.com/pod-product-compliance
Lightning Source LLC
Chambersburg PA
CBHW080423240526
45472CB00022B/2220